$$\frac{hho\,\mathcal{X}}{0\,0}$$

CITIES OF PAUL

CITIES OF PAUL

Beacons of the Past rekindled for the Present

BY

WILLIAM BURNET WRIGHT

AUTHOR OF "ANCIENT CITIES, FROM THE DAWN TO
THE DAYLIGHT"

x

BOSTON AND NEW YORK
HOUGHTON, MIFFLIN & COMPANY
The Riverside Press, Cambridge
1905

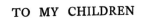

TO MY CHILDREN

TO THE READER

THE diseases which infected all and ruined most of the cities mentioned in this book are not strangers among us. Political rings more insolent and more rapacious than that which plundered Tarsus are objects familiar to most Americans. The greed that turned into bandits the merchants of Corinth has perverted into depredators upon the community some, at least, of those soldiers without uniforms, whose legitimate business is to defend it from hunger and cold and nakedness. Roman contempt for the helpless slave has reappeared in that brutal indifference to the public welfare shown alike by syndicates of capital and combinations of labor; upper and nether millstones grinding the rest of us between them. Many trustees of enormous revenues confided to their charge for use in visiting the fatherless and widows in their affliction do not appear to have kept themselves unspotted from the world. The taint of the spirit which degraded Greek athletics is said to have touched even our universities. These, and other facts of which the effects are traced in these pages, appear, when illumined by the " Beacons of the Past," sufficiently alarming.

But there are signs of better things to come. A general insurrection against the usurped authority of spoilsmen and the forces of organized injustice has begun. It is gaining strength. Shifty politicians who have led the people by the tinkle of party names as bell-wethers lead sheep are bewildered by a new spirit with which their experience has not taught them how to cope. In many places they have seen themselves disregarded, and their henchmen outvoted in favor of what they have despised as "Sunday-school politics." The men whose popularity to-day eclipses all other reputations are those who have shown the disposition and ability which enabled Gideon to cast down the altar of corruption that defiled his home, and to break the power of its ministers.

Young men — in whom is the hope of the Republic — are enlisting with unselfish enthusiasm and in constantly increasing numbers to fight the good fight. The corrupters are hard pressed. The only dangers honest men need fear are those which arise when enthusiasm grows weary in well doing. Against that temptation may this little book help to brace true patriots by leading them in hours of discouragement or apparent defeat to ponder the experiences of that preëminent reformer who, when he was weak, was strong because he felt that he could "do all things" through the One who strengthened him.

CONTENTS

CITIES OF PAUL

I

TARSUS

AT the angle formed by the junction of
the Syrian coast-line with that of Asia
Minor the land is dented by a small
thimble-shaped inlet tilting east of north.
Upon its shore the Phœnicians built a
city, after which it was called " the Gulf
of Myriandros." The Greeks built another, which gave it the name of Issus.
A third, founded by Alexander to commemorate his conquest of Darius, caused
it to be permanently designated " the
Gulf of Alexander."

Even Celtic irreverence would scarcely
venture to clip the august name at which
the ancient world grew pale into "Sandy
the Great." But " Iskander" is Turk-

ish for "Alexander." There seems no harm in docking that. "Alexander's Gulf" has therefore come down to us in the undignified form of "Scandaroon."

Stretching westward from this inlet for sixty miles and extending thirty in average width, inclosed on the north and west by rugged mountains and on the south by the Mediterranean Sea, lies the Cilician plain. Sterile now, it was once a fertile prairie. No other equal portion of the earth's surface has been rendered so famous by the battles fought upon its breast or waged upon its borders. Near its western boundary and dominating the entire region so completely that we may venture to call the whole plain, as Josephus says "it was called of old," "Tarsus," stood the City of Paul's Youth.

Three hundred and thirty-two years before the birth of Christ Persia was the one conspicuous nation in the world. For weight of influence she bore to other nations much the same relation which at present England bears to Egypt or France to Morocco. Those living at that time may have heard rumors of military preparations in the north of Greece. Compared with the kinglet who was making them, the Persian monarch appeared as the Russian Czar, before his prestige was destroyed, would have looked beside the King of Belgium. Had the kinglet been asked whither he was going, the reply might have been, " To Tarsus, for the conquest of the world ! "

Had you lived forty-one years before the birth of Christ, you might have seen in the harbor of Egyptian Alexandria a vessel loading with purple and gold and pearls and perfumes. Had you asked its owner, " Whither shall it bear you ? " the reply, spoken without an error or a trace of foreign accent in either one of seven languages, and spoken in a voice of such alluring sweetness that to resist its enchantment seemed beyond the power of mortal man, might have been, " I am going to Tarsus to conquer the world !"

A little later the Cilicians saw a gilded barge gliding up the Cydnus, propelled by sails of purple silk and oars of silver, which kept time to the music of flutes. Upon the deck beneath a canopy of cloth of gold reclined the Sorceress of the Nile. Lovely children winged as cupids clustered around her couch; fair women adorned as graces handled the tackling of twisted gold and silver or flung upon the air the costliest of Arabian perfumes. At Tarsus the enchantress stepped upon the shore, entered the Agora, smiled upon Mark Antony, then the virtual sovereign of the earth, and led him a willing captive with her jeweled hand.

Had you lived eleven centuries after the birth of Christ, you would have heard Europe clanging with arms. The ablest captain of his age, the devoutest of the

German Cæsars and — made so by that,
I think — beyond comparison the most
commanding of them all, was gather-
ing into his army the ablest warriors
of Christendom. The seventy winters
which had changed his luxuriant beard
from red to white had purified his am-
bitions and increased his authority. Ask
him whither he is going, and he will
answer, "To Tarsus, to conquer the
Orient for Christ!" Near Tarsus you
might have seen the same waters which
attacked but spared the life of Alexander
and floated the barge of Cleopatra stab
to death with their icy chill the body of
Barbarossa.

Had you been alive when Christ was
born, you might have seen a little boy
playing in a garden at Tarsus. Had you
asked him whither he was going, he could
not have told you, but we can reply,
" He was going *from* Tarsus to conquer
the world!"

The empire Alexander founded at Tarsus endured ten years. The sovereignty Cleopatra established at Tarsus lasted a few months. The army of Frederick melted away when, near Tarsus, its leader died. But for nineteen centuries the victories of the boy from Tarsus have multiplied with the years, and you, reader, whatever your creed may be, are, by reason of the civilization which has moulded you, a captive of his bow and of his spear.

A visit to his birthplace and early home will help us to know him, because the impressions received in childhood are the chisels of character and make the " child the father of the man." Passing many facts which justified the Apostle's civic pride and warranted him in calling his birthplace " no mean city," I ask your attention to those only which shed light upon himself.

I. Paul was by inheritance a Roman

citizen. His birth at Tarsus fostered in him a consciousness of that dignity more powerfully than birth in Rome itself would have done. For Tarsus, though in culture the rival of Athens and Alexandria, in commerce a metropolis, and in importance to the imperial navy without a peer, was not one of those cities in which birth carried with it the rights of Roman citizenship. The few, therefore, in Tarsus who possessed that distinction would be more eminent among their neighbors than the many in Rome who possessed it would be among theirs, for the same reason which makes an Englishman more conspicuous in Calcutta than in London. Born the equal of any subject, he was bred where that inheritance was peculiarly significant. It is not strange, therefore, that he alone of the Apostles showed at all times a sense of high worldly station. His aristocratic consciousness was ingrained.

In boyhood it became a part of himself. It was nourished by the deference showed everywhere to birth and breeding. It never left him. Witness the calm dignity of his address to the commander of Antonia; the quiet authority with which he called to account the magistrates of Philippi whom other Jews in that city would have approached as Shylock approached Bassanio; the unembarrassed mien with which he rebuked Agrippa and instructed Festus. Though a Roman he was also an Israelite, and an Israelite of the highest class. That he counted a greater honor than even Rome could confer. We shall gain a fairly accurate conception of his feelings toward Rome on the one hand and Jerusalem on the other by thinking of Montefiore or Disraeli, than whom no Jews were prouder of their Hebrew lineage and no Englishmen more loyal to their British birth. This twofold inheritance fitted Paul to become first an apostle, and secondly an apostle to the Gentiles.

II. Another characteristic of St. Paul was his keen sense of civic responsibility. He alone of the Apostles — if we may judge from their writings — saw in the duties of citizenship a miniature of what Christians owe to the new Jerusalem. It is difficult to imagine John or James or Peter saying, "Our citizenship is in heaven ; . . . therefore, my brethren, so [i. e. as faithful citizens] stand fast in the Lord." But for some reason Paul had learned to think of the kingdom of God as a municipality in which every citizen was faithful to his civic obligations.[1]

[1] Excepting Hebrews viii, 11, a quotation from one whose civic consciousness was exceedingly alert, the words "citizen," "citizenship," and their correlated verb occur, I believe, but eight times in the New Testament; five times in expressions attributed to Paul, twice in those assigned to Luke, Paul's companion, and perhaps his amanuensis, and once from the lips of a Roman officer.

This seems to be the reason. During the generation preceding his birth Tarsus had been a prey to thieves like those who have robbed and, what is worse, come near to murdering the manhood of certain cities in the United States. The " Boss " of the putrid ring was named Boethus. Mark Antony promised Tarsus a gymnasium, — probably a new one more magnificent than that which appears to have been already standing on the left bank of the Cydnus, — and appointed this well-known scoundrel superintendent and custodian of the funds for its construction, for the scamp had flattered the general's vanity by writing a silly poem in praise of the victory at Philippi. When Antony reached Tarsus certain civil service reformers who were not afraid to speak out plainly told him how plausible and slippery a knave Boethus was. Among other charges they proved that he had secreted for his own pocket's profit even the gymnast's oil. The rascal made no attempt to deny the accusation. His sole defense was this: "O most noble Antony, as Homer sung the praises of Achilles and Agamemnon, so have I sung yours. Ought I to be brought before you on a charge like this?"

The reformers replied, "Homer never stole oil, and you have!"

To those who are not politicians the reply may appear adequate. But it did not satisfy the triumvir. Through his vanity the prosecution failed. Boethus, made more brazen by its failure, stole with increased effrontery. But the reformers were in earnest. They were of a different type from those who shriek themselves hoarse over the corruptions of a ring and vote at the next election to continue it in power. They persevered, and the Providence who always helps such men helped them.

For a time Boethus treated them as Mr. Tweed treated the reformers of New York,—sneered, "What are you going to do about it?"

But the Power who, even to energetic and persistent patriots, sometimes seems dead but never is, in his own good time abolished Antony and put in his place an honest emperor, Augustus. Now there was a man of rare ability and perfect integrity, a native of Tarsus, who had been the tutor of Augustus, and had earned that sovereign's entire confidence. His name was Athenodorus. When the cry of the reformers reached Rome, Augustus appointed this man governor of their city. Athenodorus broke up the ring, banished Boethus with his henchmen, pounded the "organization" into powder, and governed the city so well that upon his death the citizens voted him divine honors, and established an annual festival to commemorate his virtues.

All this occurred in the last generation before Paul, and Paul was born before Athenodorus died. In his boyhood the Apostle must have witnessed many times, perhaps taken part in, the celebration of " Athenodorus' Day," as American boys are familiar with " Washington's Birthday."

The mention in the Epistle to the Philippians of " citizenship in heaven " seems to me a window through which one may see the battle between Tarsus and the ring that disgraced it. Can politicians who have fattened upon corruption in modern cities be described more accurately than in these words which the memory of Boethus may well have suggested, " For many walk, of whom I have told you often, and now tell you even weeping, that they are enemies of the cross of Christ; whose end is destruction, whose God is their belly, and whose glory is their shame, who mind earthly things. For our citizenship is in heaven, from whence also we look for the Saviour Jesus Christ."

III. It will be remembered how often St. Paul refers to the Greek games, not only in writing to the Corinthians, where he could scarcely avoid doing so, but elsewhere. Foot-races, boxing, hitting the mark — words from these sources fall from his pen as if they belonged to his mother tongue. Dean Howson has counted in the Pauline Epistles thirty references to Greek athletic sports, and adds that he has not exhausted the list. This is remarkable for two reasons. Paul was a Jew, and the Jews hated these naked sports because they counted them obscene. He was a Christian, and the Christians hated them because they thought them cruel. I do not remember any allusion to them by the other Apostles, though John and Peter must have been frequently brought in contact with them.

What led Paul to make so much of them? Is not this the explanation?

His boyhood was spent in Tarsus. There Greek manners prevailed. No boy could have breathed the atmosphere produced by the Greek passion for athletics without yielding in some degree to its influence. The gymnasium where the athletes trained and where the young men found a school more attractive than their famous university must have been for the youth of Tarsus a centre of interest. The games were to them more than football and boating are to the universities of England and America. Could the boy Paul altogether escape the infection? One cannot imagine the *Apostle* as a spectator watching the contests at Isthmia, yet he shows a familiarity with the minutest details of their management and practice which could have been obtained only by frequent observation. This is not surprising if in

later life he drew his illustrations from
the recollections of his boyhood, as all
men are prone to do.

Of metaphors and illustrations drawn
from Roman soldiers he has left us more
than twelve. He seems to have liked
military men and to have felt at home
with them. I incline to think this, too,
was owing to his birth at Tarsus. The
mountains north of that city and only
twenty miles away were infested by bri-
gands who made themselves a terror to
the whole Cilician plain until, not very
long before the Apostle's birth, they were
subdued by Cicero. Though I do not
know that it was so, it seems likely that
the soldiers sent to protect the city from
further depredations dwelt at Tarsus,
and that the citizens they protected
learned to value them as friends.

IV. Few passages in the Apostle's
writings have been so much misunder-
stood as those in which he appears to

depreciate intellect and learning. "The wisdom of this age," he wrote, " is foolishness with God." Many have fancied that here and in similar passages he meant to disparage the spelling-book, and all that it stands for. The most unlettered reader ought to be guarded from that delusion, by noticing that more than any other New Testament writer St. Paul honors the human intellect by appeals to its powers of reasoning and capabilities of knowledge.

When he wrote " the wisdom of this age," he was thinking of such instruction as was given at the University of Tarsus, familiar to him from his youth. The universities of Athens, Alexandria, and Tarsus were then all and more than all that Oxford and Cambridge are to England or Harvard and Yale to America. There is no indication that the Apostle was familiar with the great Greek thinkers. In the places those men had occupied three centuries before, silly professors now rattled like dried peas in a pod. They were the prototypes of those mediæval school-men who wasted their time debating how many angels could stand upon a needle's point. The problems they discussed were for the most part as trivial as they were insoluble. They cared nothing for facts. Their boast was that they could take any side of any question, and by tricks of logic prove that it was true. They were called " Sophists " or in English " wise men." It was to their pseudo-wisdom St. Paul referred. With the like of these foolish chatterers he was frequently confronted during his Gentile ministry. At Tarsus he had learned to understand them. They had filled its air with their silly twaddle. In his youth he had heard their harangues contrasted with the teaching of Moses and the Prophets. No wonder he despised them. Most readers would probably apprehend

his meaning if his language were paraphrased into, " The sophistry of this
age is foolishness with God;" we may
add, "and with men too."

V. In an age when the Jews had nearly
lost all practical belief in a future life,
and most of the Gentiles had lost it
altogether, St. Paul wrote those words
which have done more than the writings
of all the other Apostles to bring men
under the powers of the world to come.
What qualified him to do that?

Several circumstances. Among them
not the least was his birth in Tarsus.
There he had become familiar with a memorial which made him understand what
comes to communities when they lose
faith in a future life.

A few miles from the city was the village of Anchiale. Tafel traced its foundation to the Sybarite king Sardanapalus,
the Asshurbanipal of history. Here was
a tomb supposed to be that of the As-

syrian monarch. Over it stood a colossal stone statue snapping its fingers toward heaven, and bearing in Assyrian letters the inscription:

"Sardanapalus the son of Anacyndaraxes built in one day Anchiale and Tarsus. Eat, drink, and be merry. Nothing else is worth that (a finger snap)!"

We need search no farther for the origin of the quotation "Let us eat and drink, for to-morrow we die," or for the horror with which the Apostle repudiates that creed. In Tarsus he had seen whither it leads.

VI. Ægæ was another village near Tarsus. Here was a famous temple of Æsculapius, doubtless, like others of its kind, furnished with dexterous devices for counterfeiting miracles. I have no question that here Paul gained the knowledge of jugglers' tricks which enabled him at a glance to see through the pretensions of Elymas.

VII. Two other important facts may now be mentioned.

I pass the circumstance that Tarsus was the emporium for the Cilician goat's-hair tents, which it was the Apostle's trade to make, with this remark. One can scarcely doubt that the loveliest and most comforting illustration regarding death he ever used occurred to him while working at his craft. Was it not the goat-skins on his knees, as he sewed them together and reflected upon the use for which *his hands* were preparing them, and thought how soon they would wear out, that moved him to write, " We know that if our earthly house of this *tent* were dissolved, we have a building of God, an house not made *with hands*, eternal in the heavens."

But all readers of the New Testament are aware of St. Paul's familiarity with commerce and ships.

Tarsus was an ancient Chicago. Her

coins represent her as a woman seated among bales of merchandise. At the mouth of the Cydnus, twelve miles away, was the largest navy yard in the world. There, too, was the chief rendezvous, with the possible exception of Alexandria, of the Roman mercantile marine. Here were the shipyards to which galleys, men-of-war, and merchantmen — a majority of which had been built of the timber from forests close by — returned for repairs. The place was a Woolwich, a Liverpool, and one is tempted to add a Greenwich all in one. It was the pride of Tarsus. It is difficult to doubt that here in his boyhood Paul gained the familiarity with maritime affairs which made him at home on shipboard, and became conspicuous on the disastrous voyage to Puteoli. On that voyage, it will be remembered, his judgment was several times diametrically opposed to that of professional seamen, and was in every instance proved to be correct.

It seems as if the " Divinity that shapes our ends " had decreed that a man should be prepared to become the chief Apostle to the Gentiles. Therefore his youth must be spent where he will become familiar with all their ways.

He shall stand before kings, therefore he must be born and bred in a social sphere that is not easily dazzled by the purple.

He shall win a hearing from those who care for nothing but amusement, therefore his boyhood must be spent where an intimate acquaintance with their favorite amusements will enable him to clothe his message in illustrations that cannot fail to arrest their attention and arouse their interest.

He shall confound the rhetoricians who have persuaded a bewildered age to mistake them for logicians, therefore

he must be placed where a perfect understanding of their sophistries shall come
to him as an inheritance.

He shall teach two years at Ephesus,
therefore he must understand the ways
of politicians.

He shall spend much time closeted with
soldiers, therefore, for his own comfort,
he must in boyhood learn to love them.

He shall make many a voyage, and a
knowledge of the sea is for him impera-
tive, therefore he must be cradled among
ships.

He must understand the chief indus-
tries of men, therefore in childhood he
shall play among bales of merchandise.

He shall be the world's most potent
preacher of the resurrection, therefore
the most impressive picture on his primer
shall be an illustration of what it means
to lose faith in immortality.

For all these reasons he must be born
at Tarsus.

II

EPHESUS

BEAUTIFUL for situation; the metropolis and chief commercial mart of the province of Asia; preëminent in the Orient for the splendor of her buildings; worshiping in a temple which was counted the most wonderful of the world's seven wonders, and to which troubled souls from Spain to India made pilgrimages to atone for their transgressions or sent for amulets to charm away their sorrow; mother of the church which inaugurated the worship of the Virgin and placed the Madonna of Christianity upon the throne which for centuries the Madonna of pagans had occupied; cradle of Parrhasius, residence of Zeuxis, and home of Apelles, the greatest painter who ever lived; a

school of art which had no equal and but
one superior in the ancient world ; birthplace of two of the most commanding
intellectual conceptions yet given to mankind, for here was formulated that doctrine of " The Word " which dominates
Christian creeds, and here Heracleitus
announced the truth which, rediscovered
by Charles Darwin, steers the science of
to-day ; city in which Antony, "drunk
with the caresses " of Cleopatra, " madly
flung a world away," and in which Julian
was led by juggling priests to waste a
noble life in vain attempts to restore the
ruined shrines of Olympus ; the city
where Paul wrote that letter to Corinth
which is still the manual of Christian
churches ; home where Luke, " the beloved physician," spent his declining
years, and John founded the first semi-
nary for the training of young men " because they were strong ; " burial place,
almost certainly, of that disciple " whom

Jesus loved," as also of Luke and Timothy and probably of the Virgin Mary; memorable for giving name to that Pauline epistle pronounced by Coleridge to be " the divinest composition of man;" arena where the great Apostle "fought with wild beasts," and where in later years bishops and deacons in "the Robber Council" trampled each other in the name of Christ with a malignity wild beasts are incapable of feeling;— Ephesus, called by the whole Ionic race, as London was called by Englishmen, "The Good Old City" and named by Pliny "The Eye of Asia," well deserves attention.

More than to its material advantages, great as they were, its magnificence was due to the superstition which atmosphered its site with the same kind of reverence that Christians feel for Bethlehem. Ephesus was founded and fostered by the superstition of pagans. It

was long the world's chief nursery of
those magical arts which superstition
engenders. Its heart, the temple of
Diana, was destroyed and the temple's
foundations allowed to sink out of human sight and memory by the superstition of Christians. In view of these
facts, it seems significant that whether
the Epistle to the Ephesians was originally addressed to those whose name it
bears or not, it may be described correctly as the inspired antidote to superstition. For the controlling purpose of
the epistle is to show the futility in
religion of everything but affectionate
obedience to God, while superstition
consists solely in reliance upon something other than such obedience. It is
also significant that superstition is the
danger against which the letter addressed
to the church at Ephesus and preserved
in the Apocalypse warns its readers. " I
know thy works, . . . but I have this

against thee, that thou didst leave thy
first love."

To continue religious activities after
the love that inspired them has departed,
to fast three times a week only to appease a power one fears, is useless
drudgery. It perverts Christianity into
another of those superstitions it was
commissioned to destroy, and ends by
making the name of Christ a fetich as
impotent as a silver shrine of Diana.

I. Few landmarks remain to give a
correct conception of the ancient city.
The streams which fertilized her fields
have shifted their channels. Her coast-
line is changed. The canal which made
her harbor the Liverpool of Asia — the
province of that name — has long been
silted up. Of the famous temple outside
her walls not even the grave is marked.
No mound swells over its ruins which
are hidden beneath twenty feet of soil.
When Mr. Wood began his excavation,

the tobacco reserved for the sultan's use, the choicest raised in his dominions, grew above the streets where the people shouted in the ears of Paul "Great is Diana of the Ephesians!" The city where John taught has vanished. Yet it is that city through which I shall try to lead you.

Two rather steep hills, separated by a narrow valley: One of them, a ridge about thirteen hundred feet high, ran nearly east and west. From its shape and presumably also from the indentations which probably serrated its crest before they were leveled to accommodate a garrison, it was named "Prion," that is, the "Saw." The other hill, a little higher than Prion and north of its east end, was named "Coressus," or "Lady's Hill."

Tradition said that once when Diana lost her way, as the skillfulest hunters sometimes do, she ascended this elevation and inquired, "Whose place is this?" whereupon some sharp-witted Raleigh replied, "Coressus," which meant, as nearly as one can get it into English, "Thine, my Lady!" Hence the name.

A line drawn from the north base of Lady's Hill to the west base of "The Saw" would form the hypothenuse of a right triangle.[1] In the space inclosed by it was the great basin which formed the inner harbor of the city. This was supplied by water from the sea, which is now more than four miles distant, by a canal, partly natural, partly artificial, and easily navigable for the largest vessels then

[1] These are Mr. Wood's identifications. Others, as Faulkner, call Mr. Wood's "Prion" "Coressus," and his "Coressus" "Prion." In spite of Professor Ramsay's great authority, I believe Mr. Wood's identifications to be correct, because they harmonize best with known facts. The Austrian discoveries have not yet been published, but I do not see how they can affect this conclusion. In reading Faulkner or Professor Ramsay one must substitute "Prion" for Wood's "Coressus" and *vice versa.*

afloat, until it was silted up through the miscalculation of an engineer whose blunder helped to ossify this main artery of commerce and so to make the city perish of gangrene.

Around the east front of this basin, — which is to-day a reedy marsh, — the most important buildings clustered. The north side of Mt. Prion and the west and north of Coressus, terraced to their tops, were occupied by residences.

The walls circling along Mt. Prion, a little south of its crest and around the east and north base of Coressus, have been traced from a point on the south side of the canal west of the Great Basin to a point on the north side of the basin. They were more than ten feet thick; some thirty-six thousand feet in extent; were strengthened at intervals of a hundred feet by towers forty feet square, with sally ports between them, and inclosed about a thousand acres.

The city abounded in buildings which for strength and splendor and all but size equaled any and surpassed most of those in Rome itself. The population extended far beyond the walls. This bird's-eye view will enable the reader to locate the few places to which I shall call his attention.

West of Lady's Hill, between it and the basin, was the Great Forum, and close to it the school of Tyrannus, in which Paul taught. Opening toward this Forum and hewn into the base of Lady's Hill, was the great theatre. It was faced throughout with white marble, and seated nearly twenty-five thousand. It was used not only for spectacular displays but for religious and political assemblies, and seems to have served also as a bourse or meeting-place for the Board of Trade. Municipal decrees were inscribed upon the panels of its enormous stage. Many of these the spade has brought to light.

Here it was that the populace rejected
Paul and chose Demetrius for pilot.

The east side of Lady's Hill (Coressus) appears to have been a cemetery.
Here, nearly opposite the great theatre,
but somewhat north of it and higher on
the incline, was the cave in which, as the
legend ran, the seven sleepers enjoyed
their long repose. It was a cleft in the
hill artificially wrought — it is not known
when — into a sort of temple. Mark this
spot, for there is reason to suspect that
something of world-wide interest, to be
considered presently, occurred there.

At its east end, where the valley between the Saw and Lady's Hill broadens
toward the plain, the discovery of a tomb,
with the cross, the nimbus-crowned human figure, and the symbolic ox, lends
help to the tradition that Luke was
buried here. From the great theatre an
avenue ran eastward between the Saw
(Prion) and Lady's Hill (Coressus),

curved around the latter to the north, and passing through the Magnesian Gate continued north-northwest to the Temple of Diana, a mile beyond. Until the last quarter of the nineteenth century that stupendous structure was supposed by modern scholars to have stood within the city walls. Mr. Wood, after searching six years in vain for its location, discovered in the great theatre an inscription which showed him where to look, and digging twenty feet below a field of barley he found the true site.

The avenue between the Magnesian Gate and the temple deserves attention. The gate itself, the only one of the six superb entrances to the city which concerns us, was a magnificent structure. It was flanked with strong towers, and offered two broad openings for vehicles, with one for pedestrians between them. Above these, I cannot tell precisely where, was carved in high relief the figure of Nemesis, with wings and wheels to indicate that she was equally at home on earth and in air. Beneath, the name of Vespasian in due time appeared.

From this gate two chariot-ways, separated by a footway, led to the temple. The footway was covered by a decorated roof resting on marble pillars. Both sides of the avenue were lined with statues carved by Greek sculptors, tablets dedicated to renowned Ephesians, and tombs in which it seems terra-cotta lamps were kept burning day and night. Conspicuous among these was the colossal bronze representing Androclus, the mythical William Tell of Ephesus, as an armed warrior holding, I believe but am not sure, a torch in place of a spear.

The avenue seems to have been not only a thoroughfare, but to have had playgrounds for children, and it touches a tender chord to find, in digging to its level, marbles such as our boys play with and hairpins of gold, silver, bone, and cheap metal, dropped perhaps by girls who romped here two thousand years ago.

The avenue terminated at the great temple built on the site of that which was burned on the night of Alexander's birth. It was the work of the same architect who designed Alexandria. The grandeur of his conceptions was revealed, not only in the Pharos of that city, but even more impressively in his request for permission to hew Mt. Athos into a statue of Alexander which should represent him holding in his right hand a city large enough for ten thousand inhabitants and in his left a lake into which all the streams of the mountain should be gathered and poured — a perpetual cataract — into the Ægean. There is hopeless uncertainty about the artist's name. Strabo calls him Cheirocrates; Plutarch calls him Stasicrates; another author calls him Deinocrates, and still another Chersiphron. No one knows which name to accept. It is significant of many things that if asked who destroyed the famous temple every schoolboy would reply, " Herostratos was that scamp," [1] though no scholar living can tell who rebuilt it. That, too, in spite of the fact that because the incendiary fired the temple to make his name remembered by posterity, the city decreed that no one should speak his name under penalty of death.

All men know that Cain was the first murderer. But who was the first physician? Let him who can reply.

A glance at the temple revealed a forest of white marble columns surrounded by beautiful gardens. The shafts, each sixty feet in height and hewn from a single block, stood upon drums carved in high

[1] De Quincey.

relief by the skillfulest Greek artists. The columns were the gifts of kings.

The heart of this marble forest was the Shrine of Diana. In that shrine stood the image of the goddess in pure gold, and beside it, shaped into the semblance or rather the suggestion of a human figure, the meteor stone "which fell from heaven."

But these were not the only treasures of the temple. It contained statues in gold and silver of Egyptian Isis, Phrygian Cybele, Syrian Astarte, and the supreme female deities of other nations, so that worshipers from far and near, finding within its precincts the objects they adored, were made to feel as a devout Roman Catholic feels before the shrine of the Madonna. The temple was also rich in works by Praxiteles and other sculptors inferior to him alone. It contained a gallery of paintings by Parrhasius, Zeuxis, and Apelles. Here, among

several other portraits of Alexander by
the last-named artist, hung that one of
which the story ran that when Alexander declared it was not like him, and
Bucephalus neighed in recognition before it, the painter told the monarch that
his horse was a better judge of art than
its master. This was the picture which
moved the Ephesians to say, " There
are two Alexanders, one invincible, be-
gotten by Philip ; the other inimitable,
created by Apelles."

The temple furnished not only a
Lady's chapel to every pagan cult and
a British museum of art, but a savings
bank for the poor, a bank of deposit
and discount for the rich, a *mont de piété*
or pawn shop for the shiftless, and an
asylum sanctuary for criminals. No culprit could be legally arrested within bow-
shot of its bounds. Here, too, was the
merchant's principal board of trade.

Thus every department of Ephesian

life was so dominated by the Temple of Diana that we may say the atmosphere the Ephesians breathed was generated here. This fact should be kept in mind when we read the nineteenth chapter of Acts.

II. Mr. Wood discovered in the great theatre an inscription which informs us that when the men who, " having seized Gaius and Aristarchus, Paul's companions," " rushed into " that place, were boys, some of them may have dropped their marbles to run toward that same theatre after one of those processions which helped prepare the way for the victory of the peddler over the Apostle. It tells of a wealthy Roman gentleman named Salutarius who presented a number of gold and silver images, each weighing from three to seven pounds, which the city voted to Artemis. One of them represented Diana holding two stags; another figured the city as a woman

wearing a mural crown. The municipality decreed that on the 25th of May,
the birthday of the goddess, these images should be carried from the temple to the theatre and exhibited there.
This decree, the name of the donor, the
value of his gift, and the route to be
taken by the procession Mr. Wood found
inscribed upon an inner wall. It seems
probable that the ceremony formed an
æolian attachment to that held every year
on the same date in honor of Diana.
The only reason for supposing it was
not is that the images were to enter the
city by the Magnesian and leave it by
the Coressian ; and the latter, it has been
held, intended solely for pedestrians,
must have been too narrow for the passage of chariots and cars. This objection,
however, disappears before the reported
discovery by the Austrian explorers of a
broad street leading through it from the
basin to the temple.

If the images formed a part of the annual procession, its general appearance could scarcely have been widely different from the following.

First comes a band of damsels clad in fawn skins, scattering flowers as they pass. Then priests in leopard skins, some preceding, some following a platform car drawn by white mules. On this the gifts of Salutarius are displayed. Next the car of the goddess, drawn by stags, and bearing, not the meteorite stone, but a golden image representing a woman with many breasts, gleaming with jewels, supported between two golden sceptres fastened to the floor of the car. Then follow musicians. After them a woman dressed as the divine huntress with bow and quiver. Then troops of animals, dogs, deer, lions, specimens led in leash of most beasts that hunt or are hunted.

At the Magnesian Gate the procession is met by young men of the city in holiday attire, and by them conducted along the south side of Lady's Hill to the theatre where the gifts of Salutarius are placed for inspection. The terraces on both sides of the street are crowded with spectators, any of whom would be greatly if not dangerously conspicuous unless he wore pendant from his neck or fastened on his bosom a gold or silver emblem, a tiny temple, shrine, or image, to mark him as one of those ready to shout " Great is Diana of the Ephesians ! " These trinkets were the " shrines " for which Demetrius bulled the market when it had been seriously depressed by the preaching of Paul.

Twenty-five thousand persons crowd the theatre to hear speeches praising the generosity of Salutarius. When these have been spoken, the crowd rushes to the temple to see the most accomplished female dancers in the world—the Elsslers

and Taglionis of their day — perform,
with clanging shields and flashing swords,
the far-famed dance of the Amazons,
which can be witnessed nowhere else.
It seems likely that Demetrius selected
for his attack on the Apostle some such
occasion as this, as Cyril selected Lent
for the assassination of Hypatia and
Catherine a saint's day for the murder
of Coligni. Demetrius was probably a
large employer of labor. His was presumably the chief manufactory of the
images worn by the people. His trade had
been damaged already, and was threatened with ruin by the new religion.
Workingmen were alarmed by the fear
of losing employment. Priests, the good
ones, were excited by zeal for the honor
of their deity ; the bad ones by anxiety
for *their* trade. Unless this proclaimer
of an " unknown God " " who dwelt not
in temples, neither was worshiped with
men's hands," can be suppressed, their

pockets will be depleted and their influence curtailed.

Thus avarice joined with hunger and superstition to prepare powder for the explosion, and a festival may have supplied the spark. Some one whispers that there is an atheist about who has persuaded many to blaspheme by denying the deity of Diana. Another adds that through his influence trade has fallen off and workingmen are being discharged. Another adds that the atheist is a miserable Jew whom even his despised countrymen have driven as a miscreant from Jerusalem. The whispers multiply as whispers do. They grow into outcries. "Where is the atheist?" "Bring him into the theatre!"

The mob, now furious, rushes thither. They will drag Paul, if they can find him, into the place where all can see him, sure that he will not leave it alive. "Some shout one thing, some another," snarl-

ing, howling, and foaming in a way the
memory of which may have suggested
the words, " I fought with wild beasts at
Ephesus ! "

III. On the east side of Lady's Hill,
in an artificially enlarged cleft, are the
signs of what seems to have been a
temple, and in later times a church. It
was the cave I have asked the reader to
mark. Here, it was fabled, seven young
men, brothers and Christians, condemned to death during the persecution
under Diocletian, fled for concealment.
Miraculously protected, they fell asleep
and slept two hundred years. On awak-
ening they came forth and found the
city converted to Christ. Thereupon
after telling their story with great joy,
they yielded up the ghost, and to commemorate the wonder the cave was
wrought into a Christian church.

But something occurred at Ephesus
— and though no one, I believe, has

ventured to say precisely where, there
are reasons for thinking it may have
been here — more important than the
fiction of the Seven Sleepers.

The " cave " was sacred to Arcadian
Artemis.

While Julian, still a youth, was wavering between the claims of the religion in
which he had been bred and those of
the Greek cult it had superseded, he left
Athens for a surreptitious conference with
Maximus at Ephesus. Maximus was an
aged philosopher celebrated for wisdom
and also for powers deemed supernatural.
He was said to possess a voice of such
exquisite sweetness that no one could
hear him speak without being fascinated,
as Ulysses had been by the songs of the
sirens. Many thought his words oracular.
There are reasons which make it seem
probable to me that it was to this " cave,"
furnished with all appliances of the
juggler's art, that the old man brought

the young Julian. Spectres of fire appeared in the darkness. They moved around him. Mysterious sounds reached his ears. A voice declared, "The gods have given you the soul of Alexander."

Trembling with awe, the future emperor made the sign of the Cross. Instantly the spectres vanished and the sounds ceased. A moment followed of darkness and silence. Then the same voice was heard from afar saying, "That sign is impotent, but it marks a blasphemer to whom the gods will not speak."

Then Julian fell upon his face and swore a great oath that he would replace the old gods upon their thrones or perish in the attempt. Faithfully he kept the oath, and it is to his lasting honor that he strove to accomplish it not by the arguments of force, but by the persuasions of reason. When at last he was compelled to utter the confession which

Swinburne has paraphrased in the memorable lines, —

> " Thou hast conquered, O pale Galilean !
>   The world has grown grey with thy breath,
>   We have drunken of things Lethean,
>   And fed on the fulness of death," —

no man could truthfully say that he had shed blood for the furtherance of his faith. The fiction of the Seven Sleepers started those fairy tales of the " Sleeping Beauty " and the like which have cultivated the imaginations and sweetened the tempers of our children ; but the waking vision of Julian in the cave — it may be where the fabled sleepers lay — helped to change for half a generation the official religion of the Roman Empire, to pervert into an enemy of Christianity one of the least unchristlike of all the Cæsars, and went far to confirm in him those misconceptions of duty which enabled him to count as a virtue his usurpation of imperial power.

IV. But the saddest form of superstition that ever raged in Ephesus was
manifested there in the year of our Lord
449. I do not refer to the worship of the
Virgin Mother, which originated from
the decree of a council held in that city
a few years earlier. On the contrary, of
all the dogmas which I disbelieve, that
one which for centuries led men to see
in Mary those divine qualities which
theologians had made it impossible for
them to see in the phantom they had
substituted for her son, seems to me the
sweetest, the tenderest, and the most
beneficent. At a time when to most
Christians the word " Christ " signified
incarnate cruelty, the spirit of Christ
under the name of his Mother softened
the sorrows, kindled the aspirations, and
when it could not extirpate restrained
the wicked passions of untold millions.
Far be it from me to brand as a pernicious
superstition the faith which enabled

Jacopone to chant the Stabat Mater in the ears of an age which was soon to see, on every highway of Europe, flagellants frenzied by fear and dying in despair from the self-inflicted scourgings by which they strove to appease the wrath of the inexorable phantom they had been taught to call " Christ."

The superstition which clothed Ephesus with infamy was the same which has done more than all others to delay the coming of the Kingdom. It was the superstition which sired the Inquisition, burned Huss, kindled the fires of Smithfield, and painted Europe many times with blood. It murdered Bruno and tried to murder Luther, gathered the fagots for Servetus, and cursed humanity with Philip the Second. It was the superstition which the prophets of Israel fought without ceasing, which Paul's energies were strained to destroy, against which Christ was never through with

warning his disciples; the superstition
that creeds are more important than conduct, and that to love God with all the
heart and one's neighbor as one's self,
is wholly insufficient for the salvation of
the soul that holds erroneous opinions.
In 449 A. D., the churches from Rome to
Antioch and from Alexandria to Constantinople were fiercely excited over a
point of theological dogma. What that
dogma meant no mortal understood then
and no mortal understands now. There
were certain party catchwords concerning
the two natures of Christ. The words
had been emptied of their meaning, if
indeed they ever had any meaning, as
completely as the word "Tory" or
"Kingsman" has been emptied of the
meaning it carried in America to the soldiers of Washington. The words stood
for no clear conception, but for a vacuum
of conception. They became mere party
war-cries.

An Ecclesiastical Council, summoned
by the emperor, convened at Ephesus.
It was called to determine whether Eu-
tyches, a teacher at Constantinople, used
the orthodox war-cry. Dioscurus, Bishop
of Alexandria, declared that he did. Flavian, Bishop of Constantinople, declared
that he did not. One hundred and thirty-
five, some say one hundred and fifty,
bishops with their delegates assembled
to try the case. Dioscurus, made president of the council, not by the vote of
his peers, but by imperial decree, con-
trolled an overwhelming majority of the
members. The council met surrounded
by soldiers who had been placed under
his orders. Blank papers were given to
the members of the council. These
they were compelled at sword's edge to
sign. Over the signatures thus obtained
the opinion of the majority was written,
and so the council speedily reached a
"unanimous" decision. It was charged

at the opening of proceedings that one
of the bishops in conference had committed an atrocious crime, for which he
ought to be disqualified. Dioscurus, the
president, replied, "If you have a com-
plaint against his orthodoxy we will receive it, but we are not here to pass
judgment upon unchastity." Before the
"unanimous" verdict was declared, the
majority filled the air (it was in the Church
of Madonna Mary) with loud and angry
denunciations of the minority. When
the verdict had been given, the Bishop
of Alexandria, backed by a retinue of
soldiers and a rabble of monks, shouting
"He who would divide the nature of
Christ should himself be cut in two;
kill them! kill them!" knocked down
his brother the Bishop of Constantinople,
trampled the breath out of his body, and
mangled it so that in three days he died
of his wounds. The delegate from Rome,
who represented the great Leo, saved

his life by flight, and the rest of the
minority — some by lying, some by hiding in holes and cellars — escaped as best
they could.

All this occurred in the city to which
every member of the council believed
that Paul had written, " I therefore, the
prisoner in the Lord, beseech you to
walk worthily of the calling wherewith ye
were called, with all lowliness and meek-
ness, with longsuffering, forbearing one
another in love." All this was done in
the city where John had so often repeated the Master's words, "A new
commandment I give unto you, that ye
love one another." All this was done in
the city where, according to a tradition
which every one of the council ought to
have known, and most of them probably did know, that same disciple had
preached until, grown too feeble to walk,
he was carried into his pulpit, and there
repeated day after day the same words,

adding no comment, "Little children, love one another," till wearied by the iteration his hearers asked him to say something more, and heard him reply, "No! no! Little children, there is nothing more!"

III

PHILIPPI

THE CITY OF THE SUICIDES

". . . Thou shalt meet me at Philippi."

So, Shakespeare tells us, the spirit of Julius Cæsar summoned Brutus from Asia to Macedonia.

The scene is not a creation of the poet. To the minute details, — of place, tent near Sardis; of time, past midnight; the solitude; the sleeplessness; the futile attempt to read; the fading light, " how ill this taper burns," — it is copied from Plutarch.

There is no valid reason for doubting that amid precisely these circumstances Brutus saw or thought he saw an apparition and heard or thought he heard it say, " I am thy evil genius. I will meet thee at Philippi." There is no doubt whatever that he went to Philippi, and that there, by his defeat and death, changed the history of the world.

Paul also, alone, in Asia, at night, saw a vision. A man of Macedonia appeared and said to him, " Come over into Macedonia and help us."

The Apostle obeyed the summons, and at Philippi inaugurated a change still more important. But Philippi claims attention not only because there the "last of the Romans" ended and the "first of the Apostles" began their work in Europe ; at Philippi, it may be said, the civilized world was conquered three times and in three different ways.

Without the phalanx Alexander could not have overcome the Orient. But it was the thousand talents taken yearly by his father from the mines of Philippi which created the phalanx.

At Philippi forty-two years before Christ the battle was fought which decided that the Roman republic should be an empire. At Philippi it seems probable that Paul planted Christianity in Europe. For these reasons it seems scarcely an exaggeration to say that at Philippi deeds were done which have three times conquered the civilized world, — once by money, once by arms, and once by moral force.

Only ruins, among which are traces of a theatre, cut in the solid rock of the hillside, and an ancient sarcophagus, which the peasants still believe to be the crib of Bucephalus, mark the site of the celebrated city, but it is possible, by combining hints from widely separated sources, to form a fairly accurate picture of the place.

It was as purely as San Francisco a creation of gold mines.

A certain mountain in Thrace was believed to be the favorite resort of Dionysus, the Greek Bacchus. Him,

the Thracian mountaineers chiefly worshiped. The mountain was also rich
in gold, which most men chiefly worship.
At the foot of the mountain was a min-
ing camp, — one can scarcely say "a
settlement," — named, from the abundance of waters near it, "The Springs."

Philip, a more far-sighted statesman
than his more celebrated son, discerned
the capabilities of the location. First he
renamed it after himself. There were several springs, and he meant to claim them
all. Each of them was therefore named
"Philip," and the whole of them "The
Philips." Thus the city got the plural
name Philippi, not because there were
many Philips, but many streams bearing
the same man's name.

Next, in order to secure an adequate
supply of laborers, he declared the place,
because it was near the sacred mountain,
a sanctuary. This soon made it a sort
of Botany Bay, a refuge for criminals

and fugitive slaves from all parts of Greece, for here the laws they had broken could not claim them.

To keep such refuse at work, to prevent their cutting each other's throats and decamping with treasure, no less than to protect their operations from the fierce mountaineers, soldiers and fortifications were requisite. The astute monarch provided both, and so arose Philippi, the treasury from which the gold that enabled Alexander to conquer the world was drawn.

We will visit the place in the year B. C. 42.

Sailing westward across the Ægean Sea from near the site of Homer's Troy, we land at Neapolis, the port of Philippi. Here close to the water runs the low range called, because it joins two lofty elevations, Symbalon, or the Link. It rises steeply. A mile and a half of the Egnation Road brings us to its summit. Sixteen hundred feet below us on the west lies a fertile plain rimmed with mountains. Upon it, nine miles to the northwest, stood the city. The Egnation Road, dividing it into unequal parts, formed its main street. The north and smaller section, triangular in shape, was built upon a rounded hill of solid rock and called "High Town." The south and larger section formed a square drawn on the base of the triangle, was on level ground, and was called "Low Town."

In High Town stood the Citadel. It was of prodigious strength, and was probably the prison from which an earthquake delivered Paul. Both sections were inclosed by two concentric walls strengthened by towers and ramparts, and leaving between them a broad space filled with gardens and statues. Entering the main street from the east by the Neapolitan Gate, where, more than a century later, Claudius placed his magnificent arch, we pass on the left a vast theatre, not built upon, but cut into the rocky hill. Walking the length of the main street and out through the "Spring Gate" or "Gate of the Fountains" on the west, we pass, whether within or without both walls or between the two I am not sure, the "Aqueduct." Here the rivulets which gave name to the city were collected in a basin which supplied it with water, and discharged the surplus into the sinuous stream of the Gangas upon the banks of which Brutus cursed and Lydia prayed. The city was small. High Town and Low Town together included less than a mile north and south by half that distance east and west. Long peace had made the walls seem needless, and the wealthy lived in suburbs which extended indefinitely south and east in a wilderness of lovely gardens adorned with statues and blooming with roses famed throughout the world for their beauty.

On the plain south of the city, amid marshes and rivulets which except for a small part of the year have long been dry, the battle that destroyed the last hope of the republic was fought. Here by his own hand died the " noblest Roman of them all," with the curse upon his lips, " May the gods avenge upon the enemies of Rome these multiplied misfortunes ! "

" We must fly ! " cried some one. " Yes," answered Brutus, " but not with our feet, with our hands," and fell upon his sword.

Cassius had already killed himself; and an almost incredible number of nobles, some moved by patriotic despair, some by selfish fears, followed the example of these leaders.

Ninety-four years had passed when Paul, summoned thither as Brutus had been by a vision or an apparition, entered Philippi. To understand his experiences there and the epistle written in view of them, one should keep in mind two facts. The first is that for some reason he felt more at home with the Philippian Christians than with those of other places; wrote to them with less reserve, more as a pastor to his people or a father to his family. The second is that Philippi had become a military "Colonia." Those born there had the rights of Roman citizenship. The cities enjoying that honor were few. There was probably no other in the world where it was prized so highly or guarded so jealously as here. When the magistrates learned that they had unwittingly trampled upon it, they were aware that they would probably be mobbed if the fact became known. This accounts for their terror and their eagerness to keep their blunder concealed when Paul, always alert to his surroundings and fully understanding the dilemma in which they had placed themselves, informed them who he was.

There seem to have been few Jews in the city, perhaps not enough for a synagogue. The children of Abraham who lived there met for worship in a " porch " outside the walls, and probably upon the banks of the stream which drank the blood of Brutus.

There is a suggestiveness in the fact that the first Christian convert at Philippi appears to have been a woman.

The original cult of the region was the worship of Dionysus. His ministers were priestesses. Wild-eyed, loose-haired, they danced and rushed to and fro in riotous orgies ; and these Bacchanalian revels, led always by women believed to be inspired by the Deity, formed one of the most diabolical features of paganism. That this cult survived in the time of Paul is indicated by the fact that one such woman, supposed to be possessed by the god, a slave girl who by her " soothsaying brought much gain " to her owners, followed Paul about the streets declaring that he was the servant of the most High God.

Ten or twelve years passed. The Apostle came to love the little church at Philippi as he loved no other. To it more than to others he looked for sympathy. It was the only one which never gave him cause to shed a tear. To it he wrote, and wrote amid circumstances which we should consider most depressing, the letter that may properly be called his " joy song," for none of his other writings approaches it in gladness of heart.

He is a prisoner at Rome. One can almost hear the clank of the chain binding his right arm to the Pretorian as he draws it over the parchment in writing. And one can read between the lines reminiscences of Philippi and revelations of Rome.

I. The battle of Philippi was naturally counted by Augustus the most important ever fought. It established the empire and gave him his throne. He therefore dignified the city with supreme honors and carved his name upon its monuments. Claudius adorned it with a triumphal arch commemorating the same victory. The incidents of the battle must have been familiar to every one who walked its streets in the first century, for inscriptions at each turn brought them to mind. Plutarch wrote only what was matter of common report when he attributed to Brutus this disquisition, " When I was young, Cassius . . . I blamed Cato for killing himself, thinking it an irreligious act and not a valiant one among men to try to evade the divine course of things and not fearlessly to receive and undergo the evil that shall happen, but to run away from it. But now in my own fortunes I am of another mind; for if Providence shall not dispose of what we now undertake according to our wishes, I resolve to put no further hopes or warlike preparations to the proof, but will die contented with my fortunes. For I have *already given up my life to my country.*"

Was there no remembrance of this when the Apostle wrote, "For me to live is Christ. . . . I am in a strait betwixt two, having a desire to depart, and to be with Christ; which is far better: nevertheless to abide in the flesh is more needful for you." Therefore he will not imitate Brutus even in his wish to die.

II. Once and once only Paul used the word erroneously translated in our received version "robbery." It is in the Epistle to the Philippians, and signifies "a thing to be snatched at." In less forceful but more dignified phrase the Revised Version renders it "a thing to be grasped." Christ thought equality

with God a thing not to be snatched at,
but certified as his by humility and re-
nunciation.

Where else on earth could that description appear so forceful as in the city
where the most important and the most
familiar event in its history had been a
battle in which the four most powerful
men in the world fought, each trying to
"snatch" for himself universal sovereignty? Where else would the contrast
between the ways of Christ and those
of human ambition appear so conspicuous as in the city where the victory of
Cæsar over Brutus was blazoned upon
arches, inscribed upon the stage of the
theatre, carved upon the Citadel, and kept
constantly in mind by the divine honors
which had been instituted to Octavius
and continued to his successors?

III. Paul, remember, was at Rome.
He was constantly in the company —
for a considerable time at least — of one

of the Pretorian Guards. They were coarse men. Their vocation kept them near the emperor. They were idle and indolent and familiar with all the scandals of the palace. He must have heard their gossip. Indeed he implies that he did by the knowledge he shows of what was going on among them. I dare only hint at the foulness with which they reeked. Nero was emperor and Nero was their favorite. That is enough to say. They must have chattered about what they saw and heard. There was nothing else for them to talk of. Conversations like this must have occurred in Paul's hearing, for if *his* friends were allowed to visit him, there can be little doubt that at a time when the Pretorians were emperor-makers and enjoyed boundless license, no one of them would have submitted to the prohibition of visits from *his* cronies.

"Yesterday all Rome was at the theatre," I fancy one of them saying. "Lady Blank had on a purple gown. When the emperor saw it he flew into a fury, sent three of us to tear off her clothes. We did it, too, and she had to go home naked as she was born." "That's nothing," exclaims another; "his brother sang a song at court, and sang it so well that Nero, who sings like a frog and thinks himself a nightingale, went crazy with envy and told the old witch Locusta to poison him at dinner. She tried to, but it did n't work. So Nero pounded her black and blue till she promised to try again. He would n't trust her alone, and made her try her poison on some pigs. It killed them in a flash. So he got his brother to dinner and fed *him* on the devil's mixture. That ended him, and yesterday Locusta was made a duchess by the old boy for doing it — the old hag!"

If I should describe the half of what was going on in the palace and among

the Pretorians around him, these words
written by the Apostle to his beloved
Philippians would seem the gasping of
one in a sewer, smothering for fresh air.
"Brethren, whatsoever things are true,
whatsoever things are honorable, whatsoever things are just, whatsoever things
are pure, . . . whatsoever things are of
good report; *if there be* any virtue, *if
there be* any praise, think on *these*
things."

IV. There is a coincidence which may
be mentioned by way of introduction to
a more important matter, as it may pos-
sibly have occurred to the Apostle.

Two women of the church at Philippi,
Euodia and Syntyche, were at odds,
seriously so it seems, for Paul exhorts
them to come to an agreement and "be-
seeches" a friend to help them do so.

We are somewhat at sea for accurate
dates, but about this time the bitter ri-
valry between two court ladies filled

Rome with scandal. Their names were Octavia and Poppæa. They were fighting each other for the affections of Nero. The peculiarities of that emperor were such that in this contest Octavia was hopelessly handicapped by the fact that she was his wife. He therefore had her murdered in a particularly gruesome way, and her untimely fate excited the compassion of the city. The incident was an *al fresco* painting of the miniature squabble at Philippi.

But there is another passage in the epistle which has perplexed commentators. It is the sharp and sudden and apparently uncalled-for reference, in the opening of the third chapter, to the influence of the Jews. Dr. A. C. McGiffert (page 388 of " The Apostolic Age ") has stated the difficulties of the passage with great force and suggested a way of escape from them.

It seems to me that they vanish at

the name of Poppæa. That villain-
ous woman, if she were not a Jewish
proselyte, was certainly a partisan of the
Jews. She was an intimate friend of a
Jewish actor named Aliturius, " much
beloved by Nero," says Josephus, and
to her influence over the emperor that
historian attributes the success of the
mission upon which he was sent to
Rome. If, as is probable, she was used
by other Jews as she had been by Josephus and Aliturius, the fact explains,
not only Paul's outbreak of indignation,
but also some of the hostilities to Christ
in Nero's " palace," referred to in the
first chapter of the epistle.

The walls of a building excavated in
1857, which seems to have been a training school for court pages, were found
covered with rude pictures and inscriptions scratched upon them with nails or
knives. Some of these express the im-
patience of schoolboys with their tasks.

There is a sketch in outline of a donkey turning a mill, and beneath it the words: " Work, work, little donkey, as I have worked myself, and thou shalt be rewarded for it."

There is another which illustrates the first chapter of Philippians. It is the rough outline of a man with an ass's head stretched upon a cross. Beside it stands a youth in the attitude of prayer, and beneath is written, "Alexaminos worships his God." [1]

Consider what your feelings would be in an atmosphere reeking with such contemptuous mockery of your Saviour, and then read Paul's words penned while he breathed it: —

" Some indeed preach Christ even of envy and strife; and some also of good will: the one do it of love, knowing that I am set for the defence of the gospel: but the other proclaim Christ of faction,

[1] For these and other graffiti, see Lanciani.

not sincerely, thinking to raise up affliction for me in my bonds. What then?
only that in every way, whether in pre-
tence or in truth, Christ is proclaimed;
and therein I rejoice, yea, and will rejoice. . . . Wherefore also God highly
exalted him, and gave unto him the name
which is above every name; that at the
name of Jesus every knee should bow,
of things in heaven and things on earth
and things under the earth, and that
every tongue should confess that Jesus
Christ is Lord, to the glory of God the
Father."

IV

THESSALONICA

THE CITY OF THE SUFFERERS

If you lay your right hand palm downward on the table, the four fingers touching each other and the extended thumb crooked upward at its second joint, the part between the wrist and the line formed by the tip of your thumb and the second joints of your fingers will serve for a map of the Ægean Sea.

At the second joint of your little finger were the Troy of Homer and the Troas of St. Paul. The north shore, formed by the corresponding joints of your three other fingers, was the coast of Thrace and Macedonia. Should your fingers here change from water into land, they would pass through those provinces, and their nails would represent

the Balkans, which bound Bulgaria on
the south.

Your thumb is the Thermaic Gulf,
and the open space between it and your
forefinger a peninsula which has been
distinguished by the grave of Euripi-
des, the cradle of Aristotle, the canal
dug by Xerxes to get his scoundrels
dry-shod into Greece, and by the largest
and most splendid group of monasteries
ever known. The peninsula is a comb
with three teeth thrust southward into
the sea. Each tooth is thirty miles long,
and the eastern of the three terminates
in Mt. Athos, the terror of sailors in
ancient times. The seven thousand
monks who occupy the territory it de-
fends, though zealous worshipers of
the Virgin, are so fearful of all other
females that they will not allow a cow,
a hen, or even a she-cat, much less a
woman, to enter their domain.

At the tip of your thumb was a city,

called from immemorial time on account of the Hot Springs near it, " Therma." It was the first European fortress occupied by Xerxes. In a later age it was renamed, to honor the half-sister of Alexander the Great, " Thessalonica." Like the triumphal arch which once adorned its eastern entrance, its introductory syllable has perished, so that it is known to-day as Salonica.

A little outside the base of your thumb, in clear view from the upper streets of this city, rising nine thousand feet above the sea, stands Mt. Olympus. Its glittering dome of snow was the throne before which, in Homer's time, Jove gathered in council the deities of Greece. Dense forests at the mountain's base concealed the Pierian Spring, beside which the Muses were born and Orpheus first saw the light.

Close to the southeast of Olympus, and also visible from Thessalonica, stands Mt. Ossa. The gorge between the two, named, either from the steepness of its sides or because it was made by a single stroke of Neptune's trident, " The Cut," or in Greek, " Tempe," is the most celebrated valley in the world. Here Orpheus practiced the melodies which drew the enraptured trees to follow him and opened the gates of death before him. Here Apollo made atonement for slaying the Python and plucked the branch which, planted beside the Castalian Spring, grew into the sacred laurel of Delphi.

From Thessalonica, therefore, the Apostle who proclaimed another king than Cæsar first saw the citadel of those shadowy deities who were to vanish before the unknown God he came to declare.

I. Having located our city, let us enter it. St. Paul would not recognize it now. Scarcely more than the site on

which it stands remains unchanged. For
a little distance from the gulf the ground
slopes gently upward, then rises more
abruptly. The ancient walls can still be
traced. They were six miles in circuit,
and were flanked with frequent towers.
The north wall formed a horseshoe curv-
ing to the north ; the south wall, in a line
parallel to the water and almost touching it, joined the calks of the shoe, which
were defensive towers of great strength.
A broad avenue running parallel to the
water wall bisected the city. This avenue
formed a part of that military highway,
named the " Egnation," by which the
Hellespont was joined to the Adriatic,
and Thessalonica was the most precious
pearl upon the strand. Just inside the
western wall this main street was spanned
by a triumphal arch, probably erected by
Octavius, to commemorate the victory
at Philippi. The arch has disappeared,
but its foundations remain. They have

been excavated, and the names of the city magistrates inscribed upon them bear the title " Politarch." In the Book of Acts the same title is given them. As that title has been found nowhere else in ancient literature or on ancient monuments, the coincidence attests the accuracy of the author of the book. Two centuries after Paul a second arch was raised over the same street near the east wall, probably to honor Constantine's victory over the Sarmatians. Not far north of the spot upon which this arch was placed, it is in the highest degree probable that there stood in the days of the Apostle a small temple for the mysterious worship of the Kabiri. What that worship was is not known. We can say, however, that the parents of Alexander the Great visited Samothrace to take part in its mysteries, much as in our time pilgrims go to Lourdes; that those who did that were decorated with

a purple ribbon; were believed to be
secured against all dangers at sea and
from certain perils on land; that the
penalty for revealing what they had seen
in the mysteries was death; and that
there is good evidence for believing that
the majestic structure erected in the reign
of Trajan was built over the little temple or shrine, which advertised to the
eyes of St. Paul the existence of the cult.
Trajan's Temple, copied from the Pan-
theon, was an immense dome springing
from the ground, and could be entered
only by subterranean approaches, as
neither door nor window broke its vast
expanse save the one round opening at
the top, through which the sunbeams fell
and the smoke of sacrifice ascended.

A line drawn due south from this
structure would have bisected the rich
and aristocratic quarter of the city.
Here stood the Hippodrome, of which
there will be matters of importance to re-

port anon. It was an ellipse of immense size, much larger than the Coliseum, but more like the Flavian Amphitheatre than the Circus Maximus. A subterranean gallery similar to that through which the Roman emperors passed to their throne in the Coliseum connected it with the celebrated palace of Diocletian.

Gardens as beautiful as those which encircled Athens in her prime and far more extensive surrounded the whole city except on the water front.

II. For more than two millenniums, Thessalonica has been an important centre of influence, and is still the second city of European Turkey. During the period marked by the most venomous quarreling over creeds which has ever disgraced the Christian church, it never ceased to be called "the orthodox city," and for centuries was the Gibraltar of the Greek empire against northern barbarians.

The little company of Thessalonians won to Christ by the preaching of St. Paul were by some cause subjected to exceptional trials. Aware of this, the Apostle wrote them a letter to hearten them in their " much affliction." He urged them to wait patiently for the Saviour. They thought he meant that Christ would soon appear in visible form and set them free by physical force. To correct that impression he sent them a second letter.

These two epistles are the earliest writings in the New Testament. They have a special interest in our time for this reason : the church at Thessalonica was composed of " working " people. The letters contained the advice of an Apostle who was also a skilled workman to such of them as, driven by oppression or allured by baseless expectations, were starting toward the excesses of a modern strike.

In the first letter, moved probably by reports which had reached his ears, he had written, " We beseech you, brethren . . . that ye be ambitious to be quiet, and to do your own business, and to work with your own hands . . . that ye may walk honestly toward them that are without ; " that is, toward the general public. But as this advice appeared to have been ineffectual, he wrote in the second letter, " When we were with you, this we commanded you, that if any would not work, neither should he eat. For we hear that there are some which walk among you disorderly, working not at all, but are busybodies." That is, " busybodies who do no business," which seems to be Greek both for certain types of " walking delegates " and for their counterparts in those capitalists without capital who are called " promoters."

III. When St. Paul arrived at Thessalonica, the struggle between Roman imperialism and the visible church which ended when the decree of Constantine wrote the name of Christ upon the pagan Sunday had just begun. The imperial rescript banishing all Jews from Rome had been issued. The record of it by Suetonius is one of the only two passages in pagan literature containing the name of Christ, and Suetonius gets it wrong. " Claudius," he says, " banished from Rome all the Jews who were continually making disturbances at the instigation of one Chrestos."

Neither emperor nor historian ever learned to distinguish Christians from Jews. Both supposed Christ to be a political agitator alive in the year 52. Some of the exiles fled to Thessalonica. St. Paul was probably mistaken for one of them. Certainly the charge urged by Suetonius was raised against him there as it had been at Philippi, " These all do contrary to the decrees of Cæsar, saying that there is another king, one Jesus." So cried the Apostle's countrymen. To denounce him and his companions as among those at whom the imperial decree was aimed would help to prove their own loyalty. Policy sharpened the spear which bigotry forged. The accusation and the impression it made upon the magistrates warned the Apostle that Christians would find in the Roman government itself, which had been their protector, their fiercest foe. The warning was confirmed at Corinth. For there, while writing to the Thessalonians, he was the guest of a family exiled by Claudius. Their conversation must have helped him to perceive the approaching storm which a few years later burst in the appalling persecution of Nero. There was cause enough for those exhortations by which he strove to brace the sufferers of Thessalonica, not only against ex-

isting trials, but against the more fright-
ful terrors of the future.

If asked to prove the general need
of the comfort wherewith he comforted
them and its efficacy also, I would begin by exhibiting four photographs of
scenes in their city.

1. The first appeared a century before St. Paul entered the home of Jason.
It shows a gentleman forty-two years old
in an upper chamber of one of the aristocratic dwellings of Thessalonica. He is
surrounded by every luxury wealth can
procure, for he is the guest of a rich and
devoted adherent. He is tall, slender,
graceful, and has the eye of an eagle.
His face, still familiar to educated men,
shows signs of prodigious mental powers.
He is writing. He has finished a letter
to his wife at Rome, another to his brother, and is inditing a third to his most
intimate friend. If we believe what he
writes, and there is no reason for doubt-

ing it, his eyes are blinded and his parchment blotted by tears. He pours out
wailings which a spoiled child of twelve
might well be ashamed to utter. The
whining of Napoleon at St. Helena seems
manly beside them. " If you saw me,"
he declares, " you would not see me, not
even a trace of me, not a shadow, but the
image of a breathing corpse. Would that
before this you had seen me dead !"

" Why did I not kill myself?" he exclaims again and again.

He interrupts his self-accusations for
not committing suicide only to upbraid
the friends who had risked their lives for
his sake. He reiterates that life has no
joy left for him ; that he is without hope
in the world ; that his grief is more than
he can bear. He walks the floor, wrings
his hands, breaks into sobs and outcries ;
not only does this, but is not ashamed to
say that he does it. For he too has, like
the cheery host and hostess of St. Paul,

been banished from Rome. He has lost
office and a part of his wealth, and the
flattery of the populace. He is still
lapped in luxury. He is among devoted
friends, yet his despair is abject.

This broken-hearted sufferer was the
most cultivated man, the most brilliant
genius then living. He had mastered
all the philosophies of earth ; could write
books telling us how to grow old grace-
fully, and how to endure the ills of life
serenely — books which are still text-
books in our colleges. He was one of
the two most celebrated orators who
have ever lived, and he had the consolation of believing that he had saved his
country from destruction. But though
a master of all the world's knowledge
and wisdom, he never learned the secret
which strengthened St. Paul to " endure
all things."

You have recognized Marcus Tullius
Cicero.

2. The second picture is, I apprehend, largely one of the imagination. It can scarcely be wholly so. There is in the Museum of Constantinople a bronze medal struck in the fourth century which needs to be accounted for. It bears the head of a common Roman soldier with the name "Demetrius." [1] Moreover, something remarkable must have occurred to start the legends which perpetuate that soldier's memory, and to enthrone him rather than St. Paul as the patron saint of Thessalonica. But even were it wholly without foundation in fact, the tale of the Bollandists would represent so vividly and so accurately scenes often witnessed by the early church as to make it worth repeating.

Scene. The Amphitheatre of Thessalonica.

Time. 303 A. D.

[1] Professor Ramsay holds that Demetrius is only a Christianized name of pagan Demeter.

The tiers are crowded. A private soldier stripped of his arms stands naked in the arena. His name is Demetrius. A ring of soldiers surrounds him. Each of them holds a spear pointed at his heart. A voice of command asks, "Will you curse Jesus Christ?"

To those far off it sounded like thunder. To those who saw his face it seemed that an angel spoke to him. For at the name Jesus, to which every knee shall bow, he kneels and a glory flashes from his countenance, while he replies: —

"Christ is Lord!"

The multitude gnash their teeth. The spears pierce his heart. But a great joy fills his soul. He knows little else, but he has the knowledge which strengthened St. Paul to "endure all things."

A few years passed and then — this is authentic history — whenever foes invaded the city, its citizens comforted one another with these words, "They

cannot harm us, for Demetrius will protect us." And when, as occurred four
times to her, the city was captured,
sacked, and burned, her streets re-
sounded with this wail of despair, —

" Woe ! Woe ! Repent ! Our sins have
driven Demetrius from us."

3. It is the year 324 A. D. The sovereignty of the world has been divided
between two brothers-in-law. Constantine is ruler of the West, Licinius of the
East. Constantine has bowed his knee
to the name of Christ. Licinius hates
the name with a dull, brutal, implacable
malignity. The battle of Scutari has
finally made Constantine sole emperor.
Sparing the life of his rival, he has
banished him to Thessalonica. Here,
after ruling half the world for sixteen
years, stripped of every dignity, impotent, friendless, without a follower,
gnashing his teeth upon the Christians
whom he dares not even insult, the de-

posed potentate gnawed his own heart till, crazed by despair, he made the futile clutch at power for which his life paid the penalty.

4. The fourth picture represents a diamond of finest water set in black enamel. It cannot be photographed. The gem is too brilliant, the setting too dark for art to reproduce. This may be the reason why it is so little known, for the facts are uncontroverted.

When Thessalonica had become an almost perfect specimen of all that a Christian community ought not to be, there appeared in it an almost perfect specimen of all that a Christian ought to be.

History can show few sharper contrasts than that between western and eastern Christendom during the twelfth century. It was more radical than that between either and those Mussulmans against whom both had joined hands but not hearts. Throughout western Europe the ideal of Christian manhood was a brutal prize fighter, who neither feared God nor regarded man, enslaved by a religion which made him tremble before an unseen being whom he called God, and whom the scriptures call the devil. The only virtue worshiped was physical courage. The only vice despised was physical cowardice.

The Greeks, on the other hand, had become a congregation of cowards. They despised the courage of the Latins as stupid savagery; considered deceit and treachery weapons which distinguished men from brutes, and though voluble in professions of loyalty to Christ, had no religion at all. The diplomacy of Rome was threats enforced by spears. The diplomacy of Constantinople was lies supplemented by poisoned wine and assassin's daggers. Thessalonica was a nest of debauched manikins, fighting each other over trivial points of doctrine as angry apes contend for the straws in their cage. Her wealth was no less enormous than her profligacy. She was more depraved than even Constantinople, because her proximity to the West had kept smouldering in her heart a superstitious worship of Demetrius which made her in some degree conscious of her degradation, and put her in the class of those who know their Master's will and do it not.

In 1185, when Norman William II of Sicily besieged the city, Eustathius was its bishop. Though incomparably the most learned man of his time, his character eclipsed his learning. In a council convened by the Byzantine emperor for the sole purpose of enforcing a treacherous and secret league with the Mussulmans against the western Christians, he had single-handed thwarted the imperial purpose. In order to nullify his influence, the emperor, with fury in his heart and flattery on his lips, sent him from court to the See of Thessalonica. There his sturdy honesty and the invincible skill with which he fought a nefarious municipal ring that had clutched the city's throat provoked an opposition which drove him into exile. No sooner had he left than the men who had driven him away began to fight each other with a fury that threatened to make their city a shambles. To save it from suicide they sent a delegation who besought him on their knees to return. He instantly complied and his return brought peace.

In religion his attacks upon superstition and hypocrisy were equally effective. His see included the monasteries of Athos. These were filled with lazy beggars, some of whom had entered them for loaves and fishes, some for the sake of being called " Rabbi." To

these he said, "You are hypocrites
from head to foot." Others, and their
name was legion, who were seeking to
earn heaven by passing their lives on
treetops, standing on pillars, coffining
themselves in iron coats, or spending
their days in caves where no ray of light
could reach them, he treated more ten-
derly. Though they were counted holy
men, he said to them and of them, "Ye
are deceivers of the people and rebels
against God. Christ said his yoke was
easy and his burden light, but ye dare
to teach that his yoke is hard and his
burden heavy. Christ told his disciples
to go into the world and ye have fled
out of the world."

In this marvelous man, who has been
too little remembered, were combined
the devotion of St. Francis, the bravery
of Huss, the energy of Luther, and the
executive ability of Loyola. He was as
far in advance of his age as Bruno was

of his, but he enforced his opinions with a tact that not only saved him from martyrdom, but made them effective.

When the Norman fleet approached, Eustathius strove in vain to make the people appreciate their danger. They would not lift a finger for defense. They seemed to despise the Franks more than they hated them. There was also, it is probable, some sincerity in their answer to the bishop's exhortations, "Demetrius will sink their ships."

The bishop's reputation was such that before attacking the city the Franks sent word entreating him to leave the place before they wreaked upon it the vengeance its sins had provoked from outraged Deity, because if by any accident he should be slain in the assault "the light of the world would be put out."

His reply was of course that the shepherd must not fly when the wolves approach.

The massacre which ensued ranks among the unique and conspicuous horrors of history.

The coward Greeks attempted no resistance. Instead of defending their strong walls, they rushed into their churches shrieking prayers to Demetrius or increasing the panic by their cries "Woe! woe! Demetrius has forsaken us!"

The Norman soldiers spared neither sex nor age. There have been few manifestations of the devilishness of religious animosities equal to the following. Franks and Greeks each counted the other heretics. The Greek Church declared itself the true New Jerusalem. The Franks mocked that claim. To ridicule it, probably informed by their priests of the words in the Apocalypse "without are dogs and sorcerers," the soldiers gathered around the churches in which the quaking fugitives were

supplicating the God in whose name
these same soldiers were fighting; stood
for a while in mocking irony barking
like dogs, then rushed in and slaughtered the suppliants before their altars.

During these horrors, Eustathius, commanding, entreating, catching arms uplifted to strike, throwing himself as a
shield before the defenseless, seemed
almost omnipresent; and though the
death work lasted three hours, no accident harmed him, and when the mur-
derers paused to breathe, his eloquence
moved their leaders to stop the massacre and accept a ransom for the city.

IV. The lamentations of Cicero, the
triumph of Demetrius, the despair of
Licinius, and the heroism of Eustathius
illustrate the universal need of guidance
to that source of strength to which St.
Paul pointed eight times in his two short
letters to the Thessalonians. But they
are, among the facts which justify the title

of this paper, as drops in a gallon of misery.

During four centuries Thessalonica was the main bulwark of the Byzantine Empire in Saracenic, Gothic, and Sclavonic wars. Almost constantly under fire, she bore the brunt of those invasions. She was captured, pillaged, burned, by Egyptians, Latins, Turks. Twice she was razed almost to the ground. Yet after every devastation she revived as a plant in spring. When in 904 A. D., after sacking and burning her, the Arabs of the Nile carried twenty-two thousand of her choicest youths and maidens into slavery, it seemed that she must cease to be. But though cast down she was not destroyed, and two centuries later she appeared as rich and beautiful as ever.

Her most widely known tribulation affords a signal illustration of the fact that the Power in whom Paul trusted to bring good out of evil sometimes sends

his best blessings by the hands of sorrow.

Thessalonica had been the favorite
residence of the Emperor Theodosius.
Four years he had held it against the
repeated assaults of the Ostrogoths, and
even after assuming the purple he was
loath to leave the place. Here he united
with the church. In the winter of 370
an illness brought him to the door of
death. Though a Christian by inheritance and conviction, he had not been
baptized, but now he asked and received
baptism into the name of Him who
came, not to destroy men's lives, but to
save them. Mark how he fulfilled his
vows.

Chariot racing was becoming the favorite sport of the Greek cities. It had
not yet reached the popularity it attained
in the time of Justinian, when the colors
worn by rival charioteers became badges
dividing into rancorous factions, not

only the betting rings, but the state and the church. Beginning in the circus, it finally severed families, ruptured the court, rent the church. In the conflicts between the two parties, civilians, soldiers, emperors, bishops, took part with furious passion. Fathers fought their sons, sons slew their fathers, and women with weapons in their hands battled on one side or the other. No man dreamed of winning office in either church or state without the support of one of these factions.

When Justinian was crowned, the Greens were believed to favor the cause of his predecessor. The Blues, therefore, espoused that of the new emperor. Moved by gratitude or fear, he allowed them a license compared with which the most odious excesses of modern political thugs seem virtuous. Men wearing the blue ribbon rioted, robbed, murdered, and set fire to houses with impunity.

Five years that state of things continued. It ended in an insurrection which nearly cost Justinian his throne and his life, and was not suppressed until the palace, with a large part of the capital, lay in ashes and thirty thousand citizens had been slain by Belisarius.

This silly and fatal fashion had seized Thessalonica when in 390 her favorite charioteer committed a pestilential crime. Botheric, the imperial general in command of the garrison, imprisoned the culprit. The populace clamored for his release. To them the most disgusting crimes seemed trifles compared with the loss of a race to a rival city. The imprisonment of their favorite might mean that. Botheric refused to release the criminal. The race day arrived. The people assembled. Their favorite did not appear. In sudden fury they assaulted the garrison, which was small, slew the general, with several of his soldiers, and dragged their mutilated bodies through the streets.

The emperor was in Italy. The report of the outrage goaded him to madness. He determined to retaliate without form of law. By his orders the inhabitants of Thessalonica were invited in the emperor's name to another race in which it is probable they were given to understand that their favorite would reappear. They crowded the Hippodrome. Old men and young, women and children, rich and poor, packed the tiers of the immense inclosure. But they saw no chariots. While they waited the gates were shut. A flourish of trumpets. The spectators leaned forward at the signal, expecting to see their favorite. A very different sight met their view. Archers and spearsmen who had been concealed beneath the tiers marched into the arena. Shooting their arrows and hurling their spears into the dense masses

of spectators, they began an indiscrimi-
nate massacre. They had been ordered
to spare no one. They obeyed their
orders. For more than three hours the
slaughter continued. Foreigners and
visitors were cut down with the rest.

A wealthy merchant from abroad who
was present with his two sons offered all
his possession for the life of one of them.
The offer was accepted. While the father deliberated which son he should
save, the soldiers plunged their daggers
into the hearts of both and then slew
their parent. More than seven thousand — some authorities say fifteen —
were slain. The guilt of the emperor
who allowed and almost certainly planned
the details of this horror was more atrocious because Thessalonica had been his
home, the victims of his vengeance had
been his neighbors and his friends. Yet
perhaps no single act since the Cruci-
fixion has been overruled to the accom-

plishment of so much good by impress-
ing upon the world the spirit of Christ
as this diabolical crime.

For this deed the world saw Cæsar
himself excommunicated, compelled to
do eight months' penance, and even then
refused the Sacrament until, stripped
of every emblem of power, he had
lain all night upon the stones before
the altar of Milan Cathedral begging
forgiveness from Him "who came to
save men's lives." The sight of the
"foremost man in all this world," the
man who had power by a word to
kill or to spare whom he would of a
hundred million subjects, lying abject
as the poorest beggar because he had
broken a command of Christ, probably
impressed upon mankind the meaning
and the power of Christianity as they
had never been felt before. It was the
longest single leap toward true demo-
cracy ever made.

Those sufferers of Thessalonica did
not die in vain.

V. Thessalonica is still, as I have
said, after the capital, the most important city of European Turkey. Many of
her wealthiest citizens, though Moslems
in faith, are of Jewish descent, and their
history adds another to the mournful
memories of their home. Their ances-
tors were not the men who persecuted
Paul, but were themselves victims of a
persecution unique in its atrocity.

In 1492, while Columbus was seeking a new world, a decree of Ferdinand
and Isabella condemned to death all
unbaptized Jews found after one hundred and twenty days in their dominions. For centuries Spain had been their
home. They had created most of her
wealth. One of them offered an enormous sum to relieve her finances, which
were greatly embarrassed, if the monarchs
would adopt milder measures. While

they hesitated between cupidity and what they deemed their duty, Torquemada entered their presence, and holding a crucifix before them exclaimed, "Judas sold his Master for thirty pieces of silver. Sell Him again for a higher price and give to God an account of your bargain."

That decided the wavering sovereigns. The Jews were driven out. Robbed of all they possessed, they knew not whither to fly. Portugal was, if possible, more cruel than Spain. King Manuel's decree required all Jewish children under four years to be taken from their parents and placed under Christian training, while every Israelite above that age was driven from the kingdom. Mothers threw their offspring into the rivers or slew them with their own hands, to save them from what they thought eternal death. Dominican preachers proclaimed that the pains of purgatory would be limited to a hundred days for every Christian who killed a Jew.

Like their father from Ur, the despoiled victims of theological frenzy went forth not knowing whither they should go. But they were true to their faith. A shipload of the exiles, wrecked upon the Barbary coast, escaped starvation by eating the grass that grew wild upon the shore. Though suffering the pangs of hunger, they would not at first touch a blade because it was the Sabbath, and their law forbade the *plucking* of corn upon that day. But when their rabbi explained that there was no law against cropping as the beasts do, the ravenous zealots threw themselves upon their faces, and keeping their hands behind them, seized the green blades with their teeth.

Many of the exiles perished. Many were enslaved at the ports where they sought refuge. A considerable number fled to Thessalonica. Here they were treated with a humanity that met them nowhere else. Kind treatment in time melted away the zeal which persecution had intensified as icebergs are melted when they drift into tropic seas; and the descendants of the Spanish refugees gradually adopted the faith of their bene-factors.

Of all the cities mentioned in the New Testament, Thessalonica is the most striking illustration of the Master's words, " Blessed are they that mourn." No other of them all has suffered so much, yet she is the only one which holds to-day a position of relative im-portance equal to that she occupied when the words were spoken.

V

OLD CORINTH

THE CITY OF THE ATHLETES

The Acropolis or Citadel of Athens was a quadrangular mass of rock rising a hundred and fifty feet sheer on every side except the west. The length of its leveled top, a thousand feet from east to west, measured twice the width. Midway upon the northern verge the Ectheum, a temple to Athena, presented the most faultless specimen of Ionic grace the world has seen. Directly opposite, upon the southern verge, and dedicated to the same divinity, the Parthenon embodied the supreme achievement of Doric art.

Both buildings fronted the rising sun. The space between them was, as the whole of the Acropolis, covered thickly with statues so lovely that a torso or even an arm from one of them is counted a treasure in modern museums.

Raised by a lofty pedestal above this forest of sculpture, midway between her two temples, and towering above them, seventy feet in height, cast by Phidias from the spoils of Marathon, facing westward to overlook the city that trusted in her care, armed with helmet, shield, and spear to protect its people, stood the bronze colossus of Athena, the goddess of the mind.

Fifty-six miles to the west and plainly visible through the clear air of Greece, was the Acrocorinthus, or Citadel of Corinth.

Upon its crest, dominating that city as Athena dominated Athens, stood the temple and statue of Aphrodite, the goddess of the body.

The deity of Athens glancing scornfully at the deity of Corinth seemed to

[1] Wright's *Ancient Cities*, p. 155.

say, " Seek first the powers of the intellect as my Athenians do, and all things needful shall be added unto you."

The deity of Corinth, flashing back the scornful glance in sunny smiles, seemed to reply, " Seek first the pleasures of the body — what ye shall eat and what ye shall drink and wherewithal ye shall be clothed — and all things needful shall be yours."

Athens, loyal to her creed as the magnet to the pole, ended in midnight darkness, but left for her memorial a cluster of names, poets, philosophers, orators, and artists, unapproached for brilliancy in the annals of our race.

Corinth, no less loyal to her creed, ended in ruin still more complete, and left as her legacy only a shameful night unstarred by the name of a poet or philosopher, scarcely of an artist or an orator, bright enough to hold the attention of mankind ; and — what Americans cannot afford to forget — though she was the wealthiest city of Greece, peopled by merchant princes more magnificent than Tyre ever saw, the only one of her citizens whose name is still familiar was that penniless genius who had not where to lay his head, and yet when the emperor of the world asked him "What can I do for you?" was said to have replied, "You can get out of my sunlight."

The histories of Athens and of Corinth declare that intellectual power and material prosperity are alike unable to preserve communities which do not obey the voice which said to them, as it said to Jerusalem, "Seek first righteousness, and all things needful shall be added unto you."

The fate of Athens I have traced in another paper.[1] The ruin of old Corinth was more sudden and complete.

[1] *Ancient Cities.*

The Mediterranean, gnawing out from the west the long and narrow Gulf of Corinth, and from the southeast the broader and shorter Saronic Gulf, has nearly bitten Greece in two. Between these gulfs a bar of rock three miles thick holds its almost severed parts together. The slight vessels of antiquity, placed on frames with wooden rollers, were drawn across the narrow bar, and for this reason it was named "the place over which things go," or in Greek, "the isthmus." Nature marked the spot for a commercial centre. While commerce was confined almost wholly to the Mediterranean, the "isthmus" was relatively more important than is Suez or Panama to-day.

Eight miles west of its narrowest part the isthmus broadens to six miles. There stood Corinth. It was older than Sparta, older than Athens. To picture its appearance think of a heavily, puffily upholstered chair with a very high back, a very low seat, and no arms, so placed as to face a little east of north. The back is a huge crag, rising, not sheer but steep, more than eighteen hundred feet. The seat is a gently sloping mass of rock thrust from the crag two hundred feet above its base. Upon this seat the city rested, and its walls, including back of crag and seat of rock, were about ten miles in circuit. Upon the summit of the crag which formed the Acrocorinthus rested a dainty temple of Aphrodite. Near it, probably within the temple precincts, a spring of water named Peirene formed, with Siloa and Castalia, one of the three most celebrated fountains the world has known. The entire water supply of the city till the time of Hadrian came from this mountainous crag. Its waters were artificially conducted to three different reservoirs, each inclosed and roofed with marble, and

probably bearing at one or another time
the name "Peirene." Two of these
have been located by Professor Richardson.

Hadrian supplied a fourth reservoir
from a more distant source, and placed
upon its brink a winged horse of bronze
pouring the stream through an uplifted
ivory hoof. The significance of this device we shall presently consider.

The entire crag or mountain was terraced and planted with trees and flowers,
so that viewed from the north it re-
sembled an immense bouquet, out of
which peered statues in marble and
bronze, marking the winding road that
led to the temple on its summit. A
broad way running north between military walls joined the city with Lechæum,
its harbor on the Corinthian Gulf; and a
second spacious avenue to the southeast,
bordered by pine groves, thick set with
stately mausoleums and statues of the

dead, conducted to Cenchreæ, the harbor on the Saronic Gulf. Tombs of men honored in their day abounded here, but the only personalities which gave it a distinction, still remembered, were two foreigners, — the pauper Diogenes, already mentioned, who, though he drank water only, lived in an empty wine cask at one end of the avenue, and a workingman, a tent-maker, who passed some months at the other.

The harbor of Cenchreæ lay between two rocky promontories, each of which was crowned by a temple. A colossal bronze of the Greek Neptune, holding in one hand a trident and in the other a dolphin, rose from the water between them. At Cenchreæ lived the lady Phœbe, who carried from Corinth the Epistle to the Romans. But what gave earliest and widest celebrity to Corinth remains to be told.

We are sitting in the armless chair,

facing nearly north, the Temple of Venus, like a finial ornament, high overhead. Extending the left hand a mile and a half before us, we dip our fingers at Lechæum in the Corinthian Gulf. Reaching the right arm seven miles southeast, we shake hands with Phœbe at Cenchreæ. Turn your head halfway to the right and note what is between your arms.

From gulf to gulf, eight miles away, curves the boundary. It is a military wall built to keep Xerxes out of southern Greece, and called " The Isthmian." Just inside it is the great Temple of Neptune, and near the latter the buildings used for the Isthmian games. The avenue leading to it is fringed on one side by a row of pine trees, on the other by a row of statues facing them. These grow longer every two years, for they are memorials of the victors in the biennial competitions. Next to having his statue placed at Olympia, the highest ambition of a Greek youth is to have it here. If he wins the prize at Olympia in running, boxing, wrestling, poetry, or music, his native city will proclaim a holiday to welcome him home. A breach will be made in its walls for him to enter, and when he has passed through it will be closed, that none less worthy may tread in his steps. Though he will hence-forth belong to the highest aristocracy of his country, his most valued reward will be the knowledge that his statue stands in the sacred grove of Olympia. Second only to this was the glory of the victor at Isthmia.

The history of Corinth shows no less vividly than the history of Israel the efforts of the unseen powers to save a community from its peculiar dangers, and the appalling obstinacy with which those efforts may be resisted. Before our Scriptures had been written Corinth

received her bible. In form it was un-
like ours; in substance it was similar.
How it was given, when or through
whom, no one knows.. But it was there,
and it was adapted more accurately than
our Bible to the needs and conditions
of her people. Its chapters were painted
in pictures or carved in statues which
all men saw, and sung in hymns which
all men heard. By such means its contents were made more familiar to the
inhabitants of Corinth than are the contents of our Scriptures to the people
of Christendom. It warned them with
tremendous power to cast off the sins
they cherished, and exhorted them with
equal urgency to cherish the virtues
they rejected.

The temptations of Corinth were
those which assail with special force
commercial peoples. All her wealth, and
she was the wealthiest of Greek cities,
came from commerce. Merchants were

her princes. As in America, business men were her sovereigns.

The first chapter in her bible, as familiar to all her children as the history of Joseph is to those in our Sunday-schools, told the story of Jason. When Corinth was young, Jason was sent on a divine business. It was the business of all merchants. Somewhere, behind barriers almost insuperable, hung a golden fleece. In spite of all obstacles he must get that fleece in an honorable way and use it as the gods should direct. He summoned the noblest men of his day to help him. They came willingly. In the ship Argo they started upon the quest. They fought dragons and conquered them. They battled with hunger and heat and cold and conquered them. Their struggles and well-earned victories made them the worthiest and strongest of the Greeks; made them the world's heroes. Then Jason re-

tired to Corinth. He did not understand that he had been sent after the
fleece that his struggles might make him
a hero. He thought only of the gold
he had won. Having gained that, he
laid up the good ship and left it to rot
in the pine grove at Corinth, wasted ten
years of sovereignty in selfish luxury,
growing baser every year, and became
false to his wife, who in revenge murdered his children. Sinking into deeper
and deeper degradation, the hero's life
ended in the sternest tragedy of Greek
mythology. "So must it be with every
one who fancies that his business is to
get money without discerning that his
real business is to make sure his struggles after money hammer and carve him
into a man," said this chapter.

The second chapter, painted in many
pictures, one of them by Polignotus so
fine that it was placed beside the shrine
of the oracle at Delphi, described in

hymns which were sung in the sanctua-
ries of Corinth as the psalms of David
were sung in the temple at Jerusalem,
exhibited another king of Corinth. He
stands in a lake, but when he stoops to
drink, the water flies from his lips.
Luscious fruits hang over him, but when
he lifts his hand to pluck them, the
boughs spring upward beyond his reach.
He is tortured by thirst and hunger,
but he cannot die. But *why* is Tantalus tormented thus? He had been in-
trusted with a treasure of gold — observe,
it is always gold that seduces in these
Corinthian lessons — and bidden to
guard it for Zeus. But he coveted the
gold, kept it for himself, lied about it,
when required to restore it declared he
did not have it. He fancied the treasure
could satisfy his desires, but found that
it aggravated them. "The first million,
which was to be more than enough,
served only to triple the craving for the

second million, and so on and on with every one who grows careless of his work in thinking of his wages," says this chapter. Who wrote it? I cannot conceive unless it were He who said, " Blessed are they that hunger and thirst after righteousness: for they shall be filled."

The third chapter is an extract from the biography of another king of Corinth.

"Up the high hill he heaves a huge round stone."

But when he has almost reached the top it slips by him, darts swiftly down, and the weary man must begin his task anew. And who is this? "Sisyphus!" every child in Corinth would have answered. " He used to cheat the merchants who came here to trade. Some say he rolled stones down the Citadel upon them and then stole their money from the mangled bodies, and now he has to roll stones forever, though no longer *down* hill." But many a modern man who has spent his life cornering the markets and ended in the poorhouse has felt, " It is I, it is I ! "

The caption of the fourth chapter I have already shown. It was written by the Emperor Hadrian and placed where every eye could read it.

In 1896 Professor R. B. Richardson while excavating found a large number of small images of horses and horses' heads. They helped him to locate the great temple the foundations of which he discovered, for he knew they were votive offerings. These offerings brought to the sanctuary by devout Corinthians more than two millenniums ago were to them in a way what hymn and prayer books are to us. They testify that the story of the horse was rooted in the minds of those worshipers as deeply as the memory of the Madonna in the mind of mediæval Europe. And this is made still more apparent by the fact that when the city had been completely destroyed and its site had remained for more than a century a desert, two hundred years after Julius Cæsar rebuilt it Hadrian found the legend of the horse still so familiar that he placed at the new reservoir a bronze of the winged steed delivering the stream from an uplifted ivory hoof; for he knew that all in the city would understand its significance and hear it calling " Ho, every one that thirsteth ! "

This is the story written in those clay hymnals, stamped on the coins, repeated in pictures, statues, poems before the eyes and in the ears of Corinth for centuries, and finally cast in bronze by Hadrian.

A monster breathing fire and devouring men ravaged a distant land. No one could stand before it, for scales of brass

covered its body and granite was as
butter in its claws. At last a prince
of Corinth, — Bellerophon by name, —
moved with compassion for the afflicted
land, watched at night by the spring of
Peirene. In his hand was a bridle. Notice the material; it is gold this time also,
but gold used as it should be. While
men slept — it is the watchers only who
see such things — the winged courser of
Zeus descended light as a snowflake to
drink at the holy fountain. The prince
laid his hand upon the steed, put the
gold bridle on its head, and guiding by
that was carried swift as thought to the
land where the Chimæra lay. Hovering
over it he slew the monster with arrows
shot from above. Mind you, only by
weapons sent from that direction can
such creatures be killed.

Thus by the sight of their ideal hero,
whenever at market they glanced at
coins on which his image was stamped,

or walked the streets, or entered the
theatre, no less than when they went to
church, the Corinthians were warned to
use their wealth in such wise that it
should guide aright the celestial coursers
— the noble aspirations, the generous
impulses — sent from heaven to slay
the beasts that devour men. Thus "Go
ye into all the world and preach the gospel to every creature" was stamped upon
the coins with which they bought their
daily bread. But their history shows that
wherever they sent one angel they sent
seven fiends, with every Bible as it were
a cargo of whiskey, so that in Paul's age
"to Corinthianize" meant in all languages that used the word "to go to the
devil."

For the people of Corinth heeded
their bible about as much as we heed
ours — no more, no less. Two facts will
make this plain.

I. Their riches came from the sea. It

was natural, therefore, that they should worship the god of the ocean. At first they did so. Their oldest temple was built to Neptune. But they turned from the manly god who taught them to earn wealth to the flattering goddess who taught them to squander it, first in luxury, next in folly, and last in unspeakable debauchery. The Temple of Neptune remained at the base, but the Temple of Venus they put upon the summit of their citadel. There it advertised to all men that religion of sumptuous and sickening depravity for which Corinth became chiefly celebrated. That cult was the most conspicuous characteristic of the place, and from it the title of this paper should be taken if it were possible to make any truthful description of that characteristic fit for modern eyes.

II. How old Corinth obeyed her bible is also shown by the Isthmian games, though their history was not completed until she had been destroyed, rebuilt, and made the " City of Parvenus."

Those games were at first religious rites. He who taught Paul that men's bodies were temples of the Holy Spirit had long before revealed the same fact to Corinth. The piety and genius of Greece founded and fostered, in honor of the gods, these competitions which strengthened both body and mind. Only honorable men were permitted to enter them. That stadium hard by the Temple of Neptune was built by those who in contributing to its cost felt as we feel when we help to build a church. That row of marble cottages for the athletes and the magnificent gymnasium for their practice were erected by the same kind of devotion which erected the Minster of Cologne and the Church of St. Peter.

Thirty days before the games began each applicant for the contests was required to appear before a court of judges chosen from the noblest in the nation, and, after sacrifices to the gods, make oath that he was of pure Greek lineage; that he had never committed an act of impiety; that he had never been convicted of a crime, and that he had trained faithfully ten months for the event. For thirty days more he must train in the Isthmian gymnasium, under the eye of the president, an official honored more highly than is the president of any university in our country.

The eventful day arrives. The foot race is called. "They that run in a race run all, but one receiveth the prize." And what is the prize? A crown of parsley leaves, in later years of pine, but never a penny of money. His prize is the green crown testifying that its wearer has won honor for his native city, and telling him that his name will be sung by poets and his statue placed among those of the renowned.

While these remained the sole rewards, kings sought admission to the contests and the best men in Greece regarded the race-course and the boxing-ring as Paul regarded that high career which he described by reference to them.

But a change came. Neither money nor anything that had a money value was contended for at the Isthmian games. Their popularity, however, became so great that they were imitated throughout Asia Minor. The Isthmian victors were sought for as coaches. Great sums were given them for service in that capacity. They yielded to the temptation which conquered Jason, Tantalus, and Sisyphus. Victory at Isthmia was sought as a lever with which to raise money at Ephesus and Antioch. Then the glory of Greek athletics passed into eclipse.

Then came the period when the wise
and the good regarded them as we regard
the prize-ring, and when, glancing at
Corinth, they scarcely knew whether they
most despised its bullies striking with
brass knuckles in the arena, or its Syba-
rites dancing with tinkling cymbals in
the courts of Aphrodite.

VI

NEW CORINTH

THE CITY OF THE PARVENUS

THE year 146 B. C. was blackened by two of the foulest deeds Rome ever perpetrated. Both of them were wrought by cupidity masking as patriotism. The patriotism was of that kind which Dr. Johnston branded as the last refuge of scoundrels.

Carthage had been the rival of Rome. She was that no longer. Her navy destroyed, her army effaced, her condition was such that Cato's apprehensions of a second Hannibal had excited smiles in the Senate. But the merchants and bankers whom Cato despised brought about what his efforts failed to accomplish. Envious of her wealth and jealous of her commercial superiority, they persuaded the Conscript Fathers that Carthage should be exterminated. Sorely against his will Scipio was forced to destroy her. After a defense as heroic as it was hopeless, the splendid metropolis of Africa ceased to exist. Neither wall nor building was left to mark its site.

" Scipio, however, whom nature had designed for a nobler part than that of an executioner, gazed with horror on his own work ; and instead of the joy of victory the victor himself was haunted by a presentiment of the retribution that would inevitably follow such a misdeed." [1]

Upon Corinth that same year Rome committed a deed no less vile. That city also was a competitor, feared by the would-be monopolists of the Tiber, and their machinations eventuated in her ruin. It was as if England should grow strong enough and wicked enough to blot out

[1] Mommsen.

Hamburg and New York in order to appropriate their trade.

> " The mills of God grind slowly,
> But they grind exceeding small."

These two iniquities, which, when undertaken, seemed to the majority expedient, are conspicuous among the causes of the " decline and fall of the Roman Empire."

It was the absence from North Africa of a strong civilized power which enabled the Vandals to establish themselves there, from that base to storm and pillage the Seven Hills and open the door for the Ostrogoths. Had Rome dealt honorably with Carthage, there would in all human probability have been such a power when it was sorely needed. Genseric and Theodoric were the divine reply to Scipio Æmilianus, long delayed but convincing when it came.

Yet Rome was not killed by spears.

She died of the plague. The seeds of it were brought by her victorious soldiers from Corinth and scattered over the whole of Italy. Great Rome murdered little Corinth easily by a single blow, but in dealing the blow she caught from her victim the disease which killed her. It would have been well for her had she remembered where it was that Ulysses went to get poison for his arrows.

Before B. C. 146 Athens had died, Sparta had died, Thebes had died ; that is, if death is the flight of the spirit from the body. Each of these cities left a legacy of splendid deeds. The body of Corinth, like the others, still lingered. If accumulating money and using it so as to make the whole earth a pander to guilty passions while piety and patriotism steadily decay be prosperity, she was prosperous. If to fester with a moral leprosy so conspicuous that when any man in any nation between Spain and the Euphrates becomes eminent as a cheat or a debaucher his neighbors say " he has Corinthianized," be *living*, Corinth lived on, growing richer every year ; making herself a coffin of gold studded with jewels, and thinking it a throne.

It is not surprising that when Greece, forgetting the days of her grandeur, caressed the ears of Midas as fondly as Titania stroked those of Bottom, she put the wealthiest of her cities at the head of her confederacy. Corinth had money in abundance. What matter that she had little else but vices ?

In proportion as men grow worthless they generally grow arrogant. So it was with Corinth. Roman ambassadors brought her a message she did not like. Without considering that they represented swords and spears and shields and veteran legions to which she could oppose only flowers and perfumes and pictures and dancing girls, she leered at

them with senile insults; drove them
from the council chamber with yells of
rage and flung filth of the streets upon
them. Rome rejoiced when she heard
of this. It brought the opportunity she
craved. Her reply was Lucius Mummius, with orders to destroy the city which
had insulted Roman ambassadors (in
large letters) and diminished Roman
trade (in very small ones, since the sting
of the wasp is scarcely visible to the
naked eye). He did the work thoroughly.
Temples, palaces, gardens were despoiled. All property, public and private,
was confiscated. A vast number of vessels laden with treasures of art were sent
to the Tiber. The citizens were sold
into slavery. The walls were leveled.
Every building but one within their circuit was razed. The ruins were fired.

The devastation continued until the
most gorgeous city in Greece, perhaps
in the world, became a heap. Roman

soldiers tore from the walls of temples and palaces pictures each worth a prince's ransom, and flung them on the ground for dice-boards, on which they gambled for female captives. The general appraised the spoils so accurately that he issued orders, in all seriousness, requiring captains of transports freighted with pictures by Polignotus and statues by Phidias and Praxiteles to replace every object missed from their cargoes. In a triumph more magnificent than Rome had ever witnessed, the treasures of Corinth were carried to the capital. The Imperial City thought she had conquered Greece. The reverse was true. Greece had begun to conquer her. The Hellenizing of Italy dates from the triumph of Mummius. The keenest-eyed of Roman historians wrote: —

"The first result of the victory of Mummius was the death of faith and morality in Rome."

Greek manners followed Greek wealth,
Grecian luxury supplanted Roman sim-
plicity, Greek skepticism drove out
Roman faith, Greek vices corrupted
Roman virtues. Thus the incurable
cancer of which Rome ultimately perished began its work. The poison into
which the wise man of Ithaca had tried
to dip the arrows to be aimed at his enemies was taken by Roman fools to flavor
their daily food.

For a hundred years Corinth remained
a desert. No human creature dwelt on
its abandoned site. The only persons to
be seen where the busiest mart in the
world had been were paupers scratching
the ground for bits of Corinthian brass,
as fellahs and Arabs to-day search the
deserted mounds beside the Nile and
the Euphrates; for the burning of Corinth, melting the vast number of gold,
silver, and bronze statues which remained
even after Attalus had filled with them

the galleries of Pergamos, and Mummius had sent to Rome as many of them as he had ships to carry, produced a new amalgam named " Corinthian brass," which was valued more highly than gold.[1]

A hundred years after Mummius, Julius Cæsar, alert to the commercial opportunities of the location, founded a second city on the ancient site. He peopled it with emancipated slaves. They were of various nationalities and diverse languages, but from such unpromising material his genius evolved a metropolis which reproduced in coarser colors the history of its predecessor. This was the city in which Paul wrote the Epistle to

[1] The doors of the " Gate Beautiful " in Herod's temple are said to have been of this material. It is probable that the stalk of that false vine drooping with clusters of emeralds and rubies, with which our Lord seems to have contrasted himself in speaking of the " true " vine of which his disciples are the branches, was also of the same.

the Romans. For obvious reasons I call it " The City of the Parvenus." In appearance it seems to have been a reproduction of ancient Corinth so far as a stone-mason can reproduce a statue by Phidias, or a sign painter a picture by Raphael. It copied the manners of Old Corinth so far as a washerwoman suddenly enriched can imitate the graces of Agnes Sorel or a bootblack ape the courtesies of Chesterfield. The morals of the old aristocracy were more easily adopted. New Corinth may be named — I think Robertson called it so — the door-mat upon which foreigners wiped their feet before entering the enchanted land. Depraved as Greek manners became, they remained always dainty, elegant, refined. Gorgeous as Roman manners became, they never ceased to be clumsy, arrogant, and coarse. The depravity of Greece married the brutality of Rome, and their offspring was New Corinth. This was

the city in which Paul spent eighteen
months. The Judæans tried to drive
him from it by violence, as he had been
driven from Philippi, but the Roman
governor suppressed the riot, and the
mob gave its leaders a drubbing at the
whipping-post. The incident reeks of
lynch law, as was to be expected in such
a place. At Corinth the Apostle was almost mastered by a depression of spirits
which threatened to paralyze his useful-
ness. There is little doubt that it was
caused by the sight of the depravities
around him. They made his work seem
hopeless. The appalling catalogue of
vices in the first chapter of Romans he
wrote here. It is only a description of
what was going on before his eyes.

And now let us open a few of the
windows in the epistles to the Corinthians, through which glimpses of the
city may be seen. No other letter in
the New Testament is so full of local

color as the first of these. No other is so minutely adapted to the special needs of its original recipients, yet it is the only one addressed to " all that call upon the name of our Lord Jesus Christ in every place," and more than all of Paul's other epistles combined, it has served as a church manual in all times and regions.

I. Some of the allusions by which the Apostle describes his own work and feelings : —

The two strands binding the new city to the old one were the Isthmian games and the Venus cult. Through all vicissitudes except during the century of its complete desolation, when they were held a few miles away, the Isthmian games continued at Corinth. Therefore Paul was sure to be understood by the Corinthians when he wrote them that he was a boxer, not beating the air, but hitting straight from the shoulder as the Isthmian athletes did ; a runner, running as the Isthmian athletes ran. He declared that he disciplined himself as the Isthmian athletes had to do before they could be admitted to the competitions, lest while he preached to others he should become a "cast-away," which was the technical term for one who failed to pass the Isthmian examinations. Again, at Isthmia Roman gladiatorial shows first entered Greece. Therefore the Corinthians would understand the "Morituri Salutamus" in 1 Corinthians iv, 9. He declared he had been made "a spectacle" both to angels and men.

One of the most conspicuous buildings in Corinth was its theatre. Professor Richardson has recovered its site. It was one of the three objects first seen by visitors whether they approached from the north by Lechæum harbor, from the east by Cenchreæ, or by the northeast from Athens, and it stood unroofed, open to the sky. May it not be that the recollection of this structure moved the Apostle to employ the word " theatre " in the more picturesque but less usual sense of " spectacle? "

He describes himself and his fellow disciples — or perhaps he tactfully refers to himself only — as the " offscourings of the earth ; " weak, helpless, worthless except for the sustaining power of Christ. The epithet was an accurate description — familiar too — of the rabble which Julius Cæsar had sent to people New Corinth, but which his genius had moulded into a great and splendid city.

Was not the Apostle thinking of the appalling doom of Old Corinth when, in the Second Epistle, he wrote the poignant entreaty which seems to press home the whole contents of his letter, " Now then we are *ambassadors* for Christ, as though God did beseech you by us : we pray you in Christ's stead, be ye reconciled to God."

II. Note some of the allusions used to describe Christ and his church. The oldest building in Corinth was a Doric temple, of which until the earthquake of A. D. 1858 five stately columns remained. Three I believe are still erect, the only work of human hands remaining above ground to mark the ancient site. Through the effacing devastations which had annihilated other structures this temple had stood in solitary grandeur; not of course unscathed, but damaged so slightly that it had been repaired and appeared in New Corinth almost as superb as it had been in the elder city. Thus it repeated to every Corinthian who should read them the words, "Other foundation (enduring foundation) can no man lay than that which is laid, which is Jesus Christ." Every man's work shall be tried by fire as that temple has been, and if any man's work abide (as it has done) " he shall receive a reward." As is your temple so is Christ's church. It, too, shall outlast all fires.

In another way I think he repeated the same truth, though this I suggest with hesitation.

The most remarkable feature in the topography of Corinth was its rock citadel, towering behind the city and supplying all the water it had.

"Our fathers," wrote Paul, "drank of a spiritual rock that followed them; and the rock was Christ."

Attempts have been made to explain the figure by reference to a late rabbinical legend that the rock smitten by Moses, or a part of it, moved in the wake of the Israelites on their way to Palestine and supplied them with water. That suggestion seems to me absurd. The natural meaning of the word used by Paul is "cliff" rather than "rock," and the allusion sounds to me like a

reminiscence of the Acrocorinthus. As
that cliff supplies the city before it, so
Christ follows his people always to give
them " living water."

Again, the little plain not far northwest of the city was one of the most
fertile in Greece. As such it was pro-
verbial. A Greek who had a farm to sell
would be likely to say, " It is as rich as
the plain of Sicyon." On every other
side of Corinth the land was notoriously
barren. Remember this when you read
what the Apostle wrote about sowing
and reaping. An oasis attracts more attention than a prairie.

III. But the three most familiar passages in all Paul's writings, the three
which we all know by heart, are the
13th of First Corinthians, which treats of
love, the 15th of the same epistle, and
the 5th of Second Corinthians, which
affirm the resurrection of the body.
How came they to be written?

We have seen that Corinth adored the
goddess of the body as Athens adored
the deity of mind. The message given
to Corinth was this, "Worship God with
your bodies." She did not long obey it.
She soon made the servant the master,
and began to worship the body itself.
Hence came her depravities and her ruin.
Post-apostolic teachers, when they found
communities traveling that same bad
road, tried to save them by preaching
asceticism, that is, by contempt and abuse
of the body. Their doctrine was, "You
have pampered your bodies and become
vile. Reverse this and grow good.
Starve your bodies, scourge them, walk
on nails, go into monasteries. That is
the road to sanctity."

Paul said no such thing. As he had
said to the men of Athens, "Whom
therefore ye ignorantly worship, him declare I unto you," so he simply repeated
to the Corinthians their own original and

acknowledged creed in an intelligible way and urged them to obey the command given them in the beginning. He said to them, as the Isthmian games had said before they were perverted, "Glorify God in your body." "Whether therefore ye eat, or drink, or whatsoever " bodily act "ye do, do all to the glory of God." For this purpose the Isthmian games were instituted, and for this even the worship of Aphrodite was begun. Through forgetting that purpose the Aphrodite cult had become a cesspool that may not be described. A thousand sirens alluring to ruin were the priestesses that ministered at her temple in Old Corinth, and there the nameless infamies catalogued in the Epistle to the Romans had set the fashions which New Corinth followed. So far had this gone that the Apostle wrote two whole chapters for an antiseptic to the sewage which had oozed from the Temple of Venus into the church of Christ, and was obliged to bid the Christian women of Corinth keep silence even in the meetings of believers, lest they should be mistaken for priestesses of shame.

It was because the Corinthians had perverted the Lord's Supper into an imitation of the Venus cult orgies, where gluttony and drunkenness were rife, that he warned them against celebrating it in a manner so unworthy.

All this shamefulness was practiced under the name of love. How did Paul fight it?

" If I speak with the tongues of men and of angels, but have not love, I am become sounding brass, or a clanging cymbal."

"Faith, hope, love, . . . and the greatest of these is love!" The false must fly when the true appears. To discredit the counterfeit he shows the genuine bill.

We come now to the 15th of First and the 5th of Second Corinthians.

Remember that both Old and New Corinth worshiped the goddess of the body, that the Isthmian games were established to honor Deity by the development of physical strength and beauty, that the Venus cult sprang from the same root.

Observe how often and with what emphasis in the two epistles Paul refers to the body, — to its purposes, its dignity, the honor divinely put upon it, and the duty of not obeying but controlling its impulses. " Glorify God with your bodies " may almost be called the theme of which the two epistles form the symphony. In that culminating chapter wherein the Apostle turns the powers of the world to come upon the wheels of present duty, and, reading the writings of time by the light of eternity, exclaims, " O death, where is thy sting," his text is not the immortal spirit, but the mortal body. He urges men so to live that their " mortal bodies " may be, as their Maker means them to be, germs of immortal ones; spiritual bodies that shall be to these of flesh and blood as tulips to their bulbs or roses to their seeds. Thus again he recalls the Corinthians to their original creed, given them long before by the same Power who spake through his lips and pen. They had perverted the message beyond the recognition of any eye unopened by the Spirit who had caught it in the beginning.

Your bodies, wrote Paul, are temples of the Holy Spirit. If we glorify Him in them, this corruptible shall put on incorruption, and death shall be swallowed up in victory. So the Apostle seems to me to teach.

That truth, written in Hebrew literature by Isaiah, had been carved by unknown architects, and to a seer's eyes was

still legible upon the foundation stones
of the temples of Poseidon and Aphrodite.

" For we know," reiterates the Apostle, substituting for the figure of plant
life passing out of its seed shell into a
glorified body, that of a man moving out
of a tent pitched for a night into a palace constructed for eternity, " that if our
earthly house of this tabernacle were dissolved, we have a building of God, an
house not made with hands, eternal in the
heavens."

VII

COLOSSÆ

SOME ninety miles eastward from Ephesus the river Lycos joins the Meander on its way to the Ægean. Here high mountains approaching each other from the north and the south leave a narrow passage for the commingled waters, then retreat and come close together again ten miles farther east. The plain they inclose is the Lycos valley. In shape it resembles an obtuse-angled triangle. The mountains which rim it are rugged, and some of their peaks rise more than eight thousand feet above the sea. Upon this plain were three cities grouped by St. Paul almost as parts of a single metropolis.

At the northwest angle of the valley upon the mountain-side was Hierapolis,

or in English the " Sacred City." It was
celebrated for a cave of superb stalactites
and a mephitic spring the vapors from
which were believed to inspire priests and
poison laymen. Here was a great temple to Cybele which long before Paul's
day had been a centre of Phrygian worship. Here, too, in later times dwelt
Bishop Papias, believed by some —
though probably on insufficient grounds
— to have been the amanuensis of " the
disciple whom Jesus loved." Here, too,
there is some reason to think that the
four daughters of Philip the Evangelist
" which did prophesy " spent their last
days. What, however, gives the place its
chief interest for us is an uncontroverted
fact to be mentioned presently.

Six miles south of Hierapolis, at the
southwest angle of the plain, south also
of the Lycos, was a city named originally
" Jove's-town," but renamed after his
wife, by one of the Seleucids, " Laodicea."

An emporium of trade, possessing a widely celebrated sanitarium or Temple of Æsculapius, the priests of which were believed to have the secret for manufacturing an eye-salve of unequaled virtue, the wealthiest and most luxurious city between Ephesus and Antioch, Laodicea is remembered only on account of the caustic letter drawn from the author of the Apocalypse by the laxity of her Christians.

At the southeast angle of the plain, ten miles east-southeast of Laodicea, was Colossæ. It was perched upon a shelf or foothill where the Lycos had cut a gorge through the mountain ridge. The gorge, steep and narrow, bisected the city, and is said by Professor Ramsay to be two and a half miles long, varying in width between one hundred and fifty and two hundred and fifty feet. The "Royal Road" which connected Smyrna and Ephesus with Persia ran through the Lycos valley and gave importance to each of its three cities.

For a long time Colossæ was the most considerable of the three, but in the time of Paul Laodicea had taken precedence and Colossæ was comparatively insignificant. At that time it was the home of a certain good-for-nothing slave, a thief and a vagabond, and of his master, a refined Christian gentleman. This fact alone has given it distinction for all ages. Providence has used the insignificance of the place as art has employed the monotony of the Nile to emphasize the grandeur of the pyramids. Paul has brought it about that we must think of Colossæ because the name is in the New Testament, and that in thinking of Colossæ nothing shall distract our attention from two facts more important for us to know than anything taught by the splendors of Ephesus. Those facts are : —

(I.) How the Christian church was cradled, fostered, and made the strongest power in the world.

(II.) How it attacked and destroyed the most malignant social and political disease of antiquity, a disease which appeared to such men as Cicero, Epictetus, and Juvenal to be both deadly and incurable.

There are times when Christian patriots lose heart as they pause to take breath in their conflicts with the worship of Mammon. A glance backward should revive their faith.

In the year A. D. 35 the wealth, the fashion, the intellectual life of the world, all its literature, all its science, all its art, all its philosophy, all its religions, all its business, all its soldiers, all its ships, both of commerce and of war, all its amusements, all its statesmen, all its politicians, all its rulers, all its lawyers, and most important of all, its little children

were precisely as they would have been
if no sermon had been preached on the
mountain and no voice had prayed,
" Father ! forgive them."

Three centuries later all was changed.
The powers of the state were nominally
Christian ; the world's ships were steered
by the pilots of Galilee, its buildings
constructed by the carpenter of Nazareth, its costliest marbles inscribed with
his name. How did the change come to
pass ? The two epistles sent by Paul to
Colossæ reveal the secret.

St. Paul is a prisoner at Rome. Near
three hundred thousand persons are in
the great circus of that city. Some are
swearing, some are betting, some are
fighting. All are alert with excitement,
for it is race day. The most admired
men in Rome are the jockeys who will
soon appear, one wearing a white, one a
red, one a blue, but the favorite a green
cap. It is some years before the advent

of the charioteer Diocles, whose skill as a whip brought him a fortune so great that he left his son a million and a quarter pounds sterling, but it is nearing the time when Juvenal declared a jockey could earn a hundred-fold more than a leading lawyer; the time of which he wrote, "The whole of Rome has flocked to the circus to-day, and the uproar of the crowd can be heard miles away." Caligula, by spending in the stables the time he should have passed in the Senate, has made the society of jockeys more envied than that of Conscript Fathers, and Nero, though he began by pretending to frown upon that scandal, has cast off disguises and taught the populace to regard his sceptre as a trifle compared with his whip.

On the Aventine, overlooking the great circus and within sound of its turmoil, was a small house where dwelt a man named Aquila with his wife Priscilla.

They had met Paul at Corinth a few
years before, had been his hosts there,
and to Ephesus the three had journeyed
together.

And now in their little parlor at
Rome the man and his wife with a
few friends, among whom probably are
Pudens and his daughter Pudentia, are
praying for their imprisoned friend and
teacher. To human ears their prayers
would seem to float on the roar of the
circus as chips on the maelstrom. They
are praying to Christ, and Rome does
not know that they are there. But when
the races are over they keep on praying.
Others join them, one by one, until the
little parlor is too small to hold their
number. A partition is knocked out. In
due time from this seed will grow what
we call a church. It is already what Paul
meant by that name. It is like the house
of Pudens which, after being buried by
the débris of centuries, will be excavated,

and on its floor a mosaic found of the Saviour holding a book upon which is written, " The Lord, defender of the house of Pudens."

Could any vision appear to most of the contemporaries of Paul more fantastic than one declaring that the prayer-room of Aquila should supplant the circus of Nero ?

While Paul in his prison was cheered by the prayers of these humble people, two visitors came to him. One was a well-known traveler from the East named Epaphras. He tells how a certain rich man, Philemon, an acquaintance of both, has, with his wife Apphia, established in his home at Colossæ such another prayer-meeting as that of Aquila. " But," Epaphras seems to have said, " you had better write them a letter, for in spite of all you told them some of those brethren, influenced partly by the priests of Hierapolis and still more by the Jews

of Laodicea, are coming to think that
Christ is a hard master, and that they can
please him only by painful penances.
Instead of enjoying the liberty you
preached, they are acting as slaves of a
cruel lord."

So Paul wrote the Epistle to the Colossians, but before he had finished it,
perhaps, another visitor appeared. He
is in rags, half starved, and looks like
a hunted hare. There may have been a
conversation something like this : —

"Who are you ?"

"My name is Onesimus. I am a slave.
I belong to Philemon of Colossæ. I
robbed him and ran away. The police
are after me. I don't know what to do."

"Why have you come to me ?"

"I was with my master in Ephesus,
and heard what you said — and — and
I have nowhere else to go."

Some years ago my bell rang softly.
I opened the door. There stood a little

girl. She was thinly clad and shivering, for it was winter. Hungry too.

" Is this Minister Wright's house ? " asked the waif.

" Yes ! "

" Are you Minister Wright ? "

" Yes ! "

" Take me."

She was cold and hungry, and, worse than either, a lost child. She had heard, perhaps in some mission school, that Jesus loved little children, and with swift childlike logic inferred that therefore Christ's ministers must take care of them. I named her my "Onesima," for she made me understand how Paul felt when he wrote that second letter to Colossæ in behalf of the slave who knew only that he was lost, and that the Apostle was the minister of One who came to seek and to save that which was lost.

These two epistles, sent, the one to Philemon and the other to the church

which was in his house, both of them
full of affectionate greetings from the
little Christian Endeavor Society in
Rome, show how the early church, unre-
garded and unnoticed by the conspicuous
powers of the time, undermined and
supplanted them all by quietly training
fathers and mothers, masters and slaves
and little children, poor men and rich
men, in their homes and in their shops,
to try to " do these sayings of mine."
They show us how Christianity achieved
that task, apparently the most hopeless
ever set before men, the abolition of
slavery.

Outside of Palestine slavery was universal. The work of city and country
was done by slaves. They were not regarded as human. For them the laws
afforded no protection. Their enormous
numbers inspired general apprehension,
and many of the cruelties practiced upon
them by their masters were caused by the

conviction that they could be kept in subjection by fear alone. Thus, when a certain slave slew with a small spear, single-handed, a boar so fierce that the hunters dared not face it, and thereby saved the lives of some of them, his Roman master had him crucified for carrying a weapon, and Cicero remarked that perhaps the master had been a little harsh, but he would not venture an opinion. When a slave was cut into mince meat and thrown to the eels for dropping a glass goblet, no indignation was expressed by the guests at the banquet.

Two incidents which probably occurred while Paul was a prisoner at Rome may serve to show what slavery in that city was. The first, cited by Celsus and accepted by Origen as true, was this. A slave boy born at Hierapolis, the city near Colossæ, as we have seen, came into the possession of Epaphroditus, who, himself a slave, had become a freedman and was Nero's most trusted intimate. The child was weak and sickly, and his master hated him. I suppose his animosity was inspired by the inherent malignity felt by vice toward virtue. The master was amusing himself by torturing the slave when the little fellow said, " Master, you 'll break that leg if you twist it any more."

Another wrench. The leg was broken. Without a cry or the change of a feature the child said : —

" There, I told you you would break it !"

The boy was Epictetus.

Paul may have known of this, for it occurred in " Cæsar's household."

While Paul was a prisoner, a slave at Rome killed his master Pedanius. It was the law that all the slaves of the murdered man should be slaughtered. Pedanius had four hundred, many of them women and children. It was proposed to make an exception by sparing the children. The proposal called forth an impassioned speech from one of the ablest senators, in which he said : —

"We have in our service whole nations of slaves, the scum of mankind, collected from all quarters of the earth : a race of men who bring with them foreign rites and the religion of their country or no religion at all. In such a conflux if the laws are silent what protection remains for the master ? "

This protest was effectual. The law took its course. The four hundred — men, women, and children — were slaughtered.

At this time — let it be remembered in honor of the Apostle — to give food or shelter, to conceal or in any way assist a fugitive slave was to incur the penalty of death. This Paul knew when Onesimus came to him. He did not justify the suppliant for robbing his mas-

ter or even for running away. He does
not seem even to have been aware that
slavery was wrong. He had just written
the letter in which he said, " Slaves,
obey in all things your masters according to the flesh, not with eye service as
men pleasers, but in singleness of heart,
fearing God," as if he thought slavery
a divine institution. But he writes to
Philemon, the slave's master, reminding
him that the slave is a Christian, a
brother therefore, and that we are all
alike Christ's slaves and must treat our
slaves as Christ treats his. He speaks
of himself and Epaphras as " slaves of
Christ," but calls Onesimus " a brother
beloved."

To the slave he said in substance,
" All things whatsoever ye would that
men should do to you, do ye even so
to them." To the master he said the
same. Through obedience to such teaching, without help of human law, or even

protest against its iniquities, slavery disappeared.

There is a bondage worse than that of Onesimus. The slavery of the ergastula was mild compared to that of the palace. Well might Caligula have envied Onesimus. That emperor, the son of Germanicus, was the idol of Rome. When he took the sceptre the Romans called him their " star," their " darling." They offered a hundred and sixty thousand victims upon their altars, to purchase blessings upon him from the gods in whom they believed. They thronged their temples, and scores of them offered their lives to the unseen powers as a ransom for his. They inscribed his name upon a shield of gold, and decreed that upon an appointed day each year their priests, their senators, and their noblest young men and maidens should carry it to the Capitol with pæans for his virtues and prayers for his prosperity. When he ordered the heads to be removed from the statues of the great gods and replaced by copies of his own, put a gold image of himself in the temple built for his worship, and had it clothed each day in robes like those he chose that day to wear, no protest checked his arrogance. His wealth was beyond computation. He could form no wish within the power of man to gratify which was not immediately performed. Yet within the compass of his empire there was probably no other slave so wretched as he.

When it thunders this divine man wraps his head in his cloth of gold and creeps under the bed quaking for fear of the gods he has supplanted. He flies to Naples, and the smoke of Vesuvius terrifies him into spasms. Three hours of the twenty-four are the most he ever hopes to sleep, and during them he is tortured by horrible dreams. In them he hears the sea roaring, sees it draw nearer and nearer while he vainly attempts to fly, shrieks as he mistakes his own cold sweat of fear for its waters. He leaps from his bed and wanders through the gorgeous corridors of his palace. He dares not have them lighted, for to his tortured brain assassination seems to lurk behind every pillar, and light will show the dagger where to strike. He is not mad. De Quincey's attempt to prove him so proves only the insanity of vicious passions unrestrained. His crimes are his only chains. They are the furies which have built the prison from which he cannot escape. In vain he tries by superstitious rites to unlock the iron gates of his penitentiary.

This terrified man is a colossal portrait of those among the Christians of Colossæ for whose help Paul wrote. Conscience, long entranced by heathen abominations, had been awakened by the vision of Christ. How to appease it

became the absorbing quest of the neo-
phytes. Hierapolis had long been the
centre of a cult which taught that the
unseen powers could be propitiated by
ascetic tortures and in no other way.
In the whole circle of the Roman Empire there was no other religious system
which called for self-torments and mu-
tilations so unspeakable as those de-
manded by Sabazius and Cybele. The
contact of Christianity with paganism
destroyed paganism, but it also modified
Christianity. In conquering the Roman
eagles it turned the dove of Bethabara
into a bird of prey. Constantine placed
the cross above the sword, but only to
make it a more effective weapon of war.
And when Liberius substituted Christ-
mas for the Saturnalia, the rioters, driven
from the cradle of Saturnus, reassembled
around the manger of Christ. To such
dangers Paul was unceasingly alert.

There can be little doubt that it was

largely the influence of Hierapolis which opened the ears of Colossians to Judaizing teachers, who substituted forms and penances for trust in the Father and made them deaf to the " Come unto me."

The Epistle to Philemon was the unconscious proclamation of liberty to the slave of circumstances.

The Epistle to the Colossians was the conscious proclamation of liberty to the slave of self. The former was understood and obeyed centuries before Luther retaught the world the meaning of the latter.

VIII

ANCYRA
Galatia
THE CITY OF THE WEATHERCOCKS

UNTIL quite recently the province of
Central Asia Minor, marked on modern
maps " Angora," was regarded without
question as the Galatia of St. Paul. Certain scholars of repute now think that
it is not, and locate the " churches of
Galatia " addressed by the Apostle in a
region farther south. Those who care to
examine the arguments for and against
the new theory will find them stated with
fairness and force in the Encyclopedia
Biblica. I do not think they have over-
thrown or even seriously undermined
the long-accepted view. The correctness
of that view seems to me confirmed
by the facts which justify the title of
this paper — facts which show clearly

that the contents of the Epistle to the Galatians answer to the known characteristics of the North Galatians as a screw fits into its matrix.

Ancyra was their capital city. The word signifies an anchor. Tradition said that Midas found an anchor buried in the ground, built a city over it, and named the place after his find. To readers who recall the history of its people the name will seem like an oak in a cornfield, or like John the Baptist among reeds shaken by the wind.

It is the business of an anchor to stand fast against all currents; of a weathercock to move at the touch of every breeze. Yet with equal fidelity to facts we may call Ancyra an anchor or a weathercock, since it has for millenniums held a race to its place in history against forces working with tremendous power to efface it from human sight and memory, yet has shown conspicuously the peculiar quali-

ties of that race which are correctly represented by a weather vane.

"The prominent qualities of the Celtic
race," says Mommsen, quoting Thierry,
"were personal bravery, in which they
excelled all nations; an open, impetuous
temperament accessible to every impression; much intelligence but at the same
time extreme mobility, want of perse-
verance, aversion to discipline and order;
ostentation and perpetual discord — the
result of boundless vanity." "Such
qualities," adds Mommsen, "those of
good soldiers and bad citizens, explain
the historic fact that the Celts have
shaken all states and have founded
none."

Now the Epistle to the Galatians is a
protest against these qualities, which may
be summed up in the single word "fickleness." Notice a few of the Apostle's vari-
ations upon that theme.

"I marvel that ye are so soon removed

from him that called you into the grace
of Christ unto another gospel."

"O foolish Galatians, who hath bewitched you, . . . before whose eyes
Jesus Christ hath been evidently set
forth, crucified among you?"

"Stand fast therefore in the liberty
wherewith Christ hath made us free,
and be not entangled again with the
yoke of bondage."

He contrasts his own steadfastness
with their vacillations.

He asks them why it is that whereas
a little while ago they were ready to give
their eyes for him, they now regard him
as their enemy.

Thus the Apostle expressed the verdict of history.

Ancyra lay some two hundred miles
east-southeast of Constantinople. Under its modern name, Angora, it is celebrated for three things: the amount of
electricity in its atmosphere, which at

times makes a blanket seem a sheet of flame; the silky hair of its dogs, its goats, and its cats; the fact that these animals when removed but thirty miles from their birthplace change their coats and become like other dogs and goats and cats.

The inhabitants of the small region named Galatia, or the "Gaul's Country," were as different from their neighbors as is an outcrop of trap from the field of quartz in which it appears. Their district consisted of three cantons, of which Ancyra, Pessinus, and Tavium were the respective capitals.

Tavium was noted for its sacred grove, — probably a memorial of Druid worship changed to the service of Jupiter, — which contained a colossal bronze of Jove, and was to its canton, perhaps to all three cantons, what the Cities of Refuge were to Israel in the time of the Judges, or Notre Dame to Paris during the Middle Ages. Pessinus was distinguished by a temple to Cybele, in which a black meteorite was adored as an image of that goddess. Many thought that the manner of its advent had given name to the place, for " Pessinus " may mean " fallen," and " from heaven " might have been understood.

Ancyra, however, the largest and most important of these capitals, may be counted the " metropolis " or mother city of Galatia, and is therefore selected as representative of all those to whom St. Paul's epistle was addressed. They belonged to the same stock as the French and Irish, and their history is a panorama of the two most conspicuous traits of Gallic character, — that passion for *La Gloire* which mistook the bulletins of Napoleon for the oracles of omnipotence, and that fickleness which in eighteen years changed its religion four times and its government twelve.

One of the pictures painted indelibly upon my memory in childhood is that of the Roman Senate in the year 391 B. C., when the Gallic " Brennus " or " king " had broken into Rome. The grand old senators, who disdain to fly, sit calmly in their accustomed places. Their white beards flow over their magnificent official robes. The gigantic warriors who have rushed in with murderous intent, awed by the sight, sink their swords, afraid to strike, and whisper, " They are not men. They are gods ! "

My mother taught me to read in that picture the triumph of mind over muscle. She told me those Gauls were the most terrific foemen Rome ever encountered. So terrible were they that the date of their invasion was recorded in the Roman calendar as " The Black Day," and a sinking fund was established in the Capitol never to be used except for defense against them. She taught me to under-

stand why it was that the equipment
of the Roman soldier was changed after
that invasion into a fashion adapted to
resist the Gallic style of attack, and thus
was born the Roman legion, which in
due time, like Alexander's phalanx, conquered the world. She told me how

> The Roman matron long did tame
> The froward child with Brennus' name,
> And Italy's maidens long grew pale
> When Brennus' sword inspired the tale.

Though unwelcome facts have tried
to blur the picture, they have but par-
tially succeeded, and it is hard for me to
feel the gratitude I owe to those who
have taught me that it was not senators
remaining in their chamber because they
disdained to fly, but old men sitting on
their doorsteps because they were too
weak to run away, and that though the
Gauls were for a moment awed by their
venerable appearance (criticism has not
yet, I believe, shaved off the august

beards) or — what is more probable —
were restrained by pity for their feeble-
ness, they soon killed them, every one.

A hundred and eleven years after
Brennus's sword and the cackling geese,
another " Brennus " or Gallic king burst
into Asia Minor and caused a reign of
terror there. When his fierce followers
had cast anchor in the district named
after them " Galatia," they continued to
be, until their power was broken by
Pergamos, the virtual arbiters in the conflicts which were perpetually arising between the rival kinglets of Asia Minor.
They rarely made war on their own account and did not enlarge their territory,
but lived in splendor by loaning their
arms to the sovereign who bid highest
for them. To-day they fought for Pon-
tus, to-morrow for Pergamos. They
changed their allies as they changed
their coats, and the power for which
they fought was usually assured of vic-

tory by the terror of their name. The
Pergamene marbles in the museum of
Berlin which a competent critic has pronounced worthy the chisel of Phidias,
and the statue of the dying Gaul falsely
named "The dying Gladiator," which
adorns the Vatican, are memorials by
which Pergamos commemorated her victory over the arrogant Galatians. In spite
of this defeat their individual prowess
long remained preëminent. Four hundred Galatian giants armed and equipped
with unequaled splendor formed the
body-guard of Cleopatra until, with
characteristic fickleness, they took a
similar position under Herod, her bitterest enemy.

When the Gauls entered Asia they
brought with them the religion of the
Druids, and practiced its mysteries in
the forests of the Dryads. Of these the
Sacred Grove at Tavium, with its bronze
Jupiter substituted for the branch of

mistletoe, was a memorial. They changed their creed as lightly as their descendants adopted and discarded the teachings of Paul. They worshiped Cybele with a fervor which made their country her Mecca, and led a Roman writer into the mistake of thinking her priests were called " Galli " because they were Gauls. That veer of the weathercock anchored it forever in the history of Rome.

The year 204 B. C. shed a deadly gloom over Italy. Hannibal had devastated her plains, and intrenched himself among her mountains. The last Scipio of the lion's brood was in Africa. The Roman army retained for home defense was threatened by pestilence, with annihilation. Rome had passed nine days in fasting, sacrifice, and prayer, but the unseen powers gave no sign. The people had almost wholly lost heart, when an appalling visitation sharpened their apprehension into panic. A shower of meteorites,

such as no living Roman had ever seen,
descended. They thought the day of
doom had come. An obscure prophecy
in the Sibylline books suggested the only
hope of salvation. The fire from the sky
was interpreted to mean that the gods
would be appeased if the image of the
Great Mother which had fallen from
heaven at Pessinus were brought to Rome
and fitly honored there. Instantly an
embassy was sent to Galatia. Would
the priests of Cybele permit the object
of their adoration to be taken from its
shrine? More than upon their armies,
more than upon the genius of their Scipio,
the hopes of the Romans hung upon the
answer to that question.

What arguments were urged to per-
suade them is not known, but the rulers
of Pessinus answered " Yes ! "

With pomp of decorated galleys
and priestly pride the black stone was
brought to the Tiber. The most blame-

less man and the most faultless woman in the state must be discovered to receive the treasure in the city's name. After long debate the young Publius Scipio was judged to be the most virtuous man and Publia Quinta the worthiest woman. Preparations for the reception had been completed when, as Herodian reports, an unexpected difficulty arose. The vessel bearing the precious freight stuck fast in the mud. All the resources of the nation could not budge it, for Cybele herself held it immovable. What should be done? A priestess of Vesta had been sentenced to death for infidelity. She prayed that her innocence might be submitted to the Great Mother for decision. Her prayer was granted. Entering the water, she unbound her girdle, fastened it to the vessel's prow, drew it easily into deep water, and was of course proved spotless.

Without vouching for the truth of this

subordinate episode, which was probably
invented to mitigate the jealousy between
the priests of Asia and those of Italy, by
showing that Cybele and Vesta were
friends, I return to undisputed history.

Scipio, followed by all the senators in
scarlet, and Quinta, leading the most illus-
trious dames of Rome in their best gowns,
met the ship at Ostia, took possession of
the sacred stone, and escorted it to the
capital. The ladies danced before it; the
statesmen marched beside it to the shrine
prepared upon the Palatine. Thus began
the festival of the Roman Madonna
called the Megalesia. A temple of white
marble which twelve years were needed
to complete was erected for the shrine
of the goddess. An order of ministers
named from the Gallic priests was established to serve her. For six days
every April the doors of the wealthy were
opened, revealing tables laden with food
and wine, around which images of

the great gods were seated with Cybele. Whosoever would might enter and partake without money and without price. Prisoners were set free. Senators formed processions to the temple. The noblest matrons — even Vestals, it is believed — danced before them. In front of all, the black stone in a gilded chariot, to which were harnessed lions of solid silver, was drawn by priests who had bathed in blood. Slaves were obliged to keep out of sight. Plays illustrating the transportation of the image from Galatia were performed in the theatres. The Imperial City never bestowed a tithe of such honors upon Scipio for defeating Hannibal.

Momentous as the change of the Galatians from the religion of the Druids to the worship of Cybele proved to Rome, another veer of the weathercock is more significant to us.

The Emperor Augustus died in the fourteenth year of our era. During his

reign more than in any other equal
length of time those subordinate forces
and facilities which coöperated with the
life of Christ to assure the victory of
Christianity were set in order. The
Augustan was not only the Elizabethan
age of Rome in literature, philosophy,
and art ; it was also the period which is
still the most important of all periods
for the student of Christianity to understand.

Though by no means a slave to vanity, Augustus appreciated adequately the
importance of his achievements, and was
alive to the significance of most of the
forces working under him. The method
he took to perpetuate the memory of
them was unique.

The tomb he built upon the Campus
Martius would merit notice if for no
other reason than its beauty. It was a
drum of Carrara marble more than two
hundred feet in diameter, and higher

than the reach of a man's hand. Upon
the roof, which was nearly flat, rested a
cone of earth covered to the top with
evergreens, its apex surmounted by a
bronze statue of himself. The whole
was surrounded by two concentric walls,
one of bronze, the other of marble, in-
closing between them gardens where
fountains played, streams rippled, flowers bloomed, and birds sang. On each
side of the entrance, between the outer
wall of marble and the inner one of
bronze (which last was probably an orna-
mental balustrade), stood a lofty bronze
column. Upon these pillars the emperor's will, his expenditures, and those
acts of his reign which he considered the
most important were inscribed. How
priceless would this record be if we had
it! But it perished. Scarce a vestige of
tomb, pillar, or inscription remains for
our instruction. What price would be
too great for a copy of those records!

Well, copies of them may be found in each of the three great libraries of Europe, but those who placed them there brought them from Ancyra.

Augustus was the first Cæsar whom the Romans deified. When that new cult was sprung upon the empire, the people of Galatia, as was their wont, adopted it with such swift and hot enthusiasm as made them recognized throughout Asia, and by the emperor himself for its stanchest devotees. Assisted by contributions from other provinces, they built a temple at Ancyra for the worship of the new divinity, and were granted, as a distinguishing mark of imperial favor, the right to inscribe upon its walls a copy of the records on the bronze pillars at Rome. The letters were cut deep into the marble through a glazé of vermilion, each letter plated with beaten gold. Though the temple is a ruin, its walls stand. The gold is gone. The vermilion has faded or scaled away. But the letters remain, a copy in Latin with a Greek translation by its side. To the fickleness of Galatians we owe this treasure no less than the still more precious Epistle of St. Paul. There is One who can make a weathercock do the work of an anchor.

Thus Ancyra was blown about by every wind of doctrine, until under Constantine Christianity became the religion of the empire. Then of course she became a stalwart for Christ. But presently came a reaction. Julian, disgusted with the quarrels of the church, educated under conditions which forced his noble nature to become familiar with the arrogance and hypocrisy which had permeated the Christian profession, and influenced in no small degree by circumstances alluded to in my paper on Ephesus, headed a movement to efface Christianity and restore the old gods. He

had tried to rebuild Jerusalem in order
to falsify the supposed predictions of
the Saviour, but had failed in the attempt. Exploding fire damp and other
signs deemed supernatural had scared
away even those Jews whose zeal set
them digging into Mt. Moriah with
silver spades and carrying rubbish in
baskets of silver and gold, while their
ladies bore away its dust in aprons of
silk. He failed to restore even the walls
of the city which he meant to honor because it had rejected Christ. He had
not yet met the monk to whom he said,
" I am going to rebuild in the East the
temple of the fire-worshipers; where is
your carpenter now?" nor heard the
reply, " He is at the Euphrates making
a coffin for your Majesty." Though the
defeat and ruin which forced him to say,
" Galilean, thou hast conquered," were
approaching fast, for a little moment he
seemed to be moving toward success.

With the celerity acquired by long practice, Ancyra adopted Julian's views. To express his appreciation of her nimbleness, before starting on the eastern campaign which cost him his life, he honored her with an imperial visit. To commemorate his coming her people raised a bronze pillar which remains to this day. Fragments of their citadel upon which they inscribed their indorsement of his apostasy are also preserved, and the inscription is legible.

It would be unfair to omit mention of what, as far as I know, is the only specimen of steadfastness ever exhibited in Ancyra, and equally unfair to cover with silence the only act of cruelty attributed to Julian, though it has been attributed to him on insufficient evidence.

In 362 A. D., when the emperor visited Ancyra, there was in that place a presbyter conspicuous for the energy of his rebukes to apostate Christians.

Day after day he tramped the streets reëchoing Paul's cry in trumpet tones: —

" O foolish Galatians, who hath bewitched you, that ye should not obey the truth?" "Who hath bewitched you?" " Who hath bewitched you? "

The man was arrested and brought before the emperor. Brave as Paul, but without Paul's kindness or a trace of his tact, he broke forth with a fury of invective, arraigning the monarch for his apostasy and threatening speedy vengeance from the Almighty upon him.

It is a fact that Basil was carried from the imperial presence and pulled to pieces with red-hot pincers, but there is no proof that he died by the emperor's order, or even that the emperor knew of his fate until the devilish deed had been done. There is also no evidence that the steadfast man was a Galatian.

When Julian's death had ended his crusade *against* the Cross, and Chris-

tianity resumed her sceptre over the
state, the conduct of Ancyra justified
her reputation. She hastened back into
the fold.

The fifteenth century found her the
residence of Bajazet and probably the
stanchest fortress in his dominions.
Here was the stronghold of the armies
which terrorized Europe and kept Constantinople for years in a state of virtual
siege, or rather of vassalage, since she
purchased her nominal independence by
large and frequent bribes. On the plain
before the city was fought, 1402 A. D.,
the battle in which Tamerlane annihilated the power of Bajazet. Whether the
conqueror imprisoned his vanquished
rival in an iron cage and exhibited him
as a sign of his triumph, as was for-
merly believed, is uncertain.

Tamerlane and Bajazet are gone, but
Ancyra stands. The temple she reared
to Augustus, then dedicated to Christ,

and at last converted into a mosque for Allah, the pillar she raised to Julian and the inscription on the fragments of her ruined citadel, and, more than these, the Epistle of Paul to her people, tell us how easily, how swiftly, and how often she turned to each shifting wind.

If you ask "What is her religion now?" the answer is that apparently tired of change, she seems at last to have hit upon a new device to satisfy her vacillating inclinations, and at present attempts to be all things at once. For here the Armenians have a large convent where the archbishop and his suffragans reside. Here the Roman Catholics maintain four churches, the Jews have their synagogues, and the Mussulmans their mosques. And here any one who discovers an improved substitute for Christianity may hope to find it easier than in most places to draw proselytes into his camp.

IX

TYANA

THE PAGAN BETHLEHEM

SOME eighty miles a trifle west of north from Tarsus, and separated from that metropolis by a wall of mountains, stood Tyana. A small city, neither rich nor strong nor beautiful, it was before the Christian era in no way distinguished. The highway to the Orient passed its walls, but commerce never paused to make it an important market. No school of art or science gave it the dignity which exalted Tarsus and Alexandria. It contained no buildings or statues which could win admiration from travelers familiar with the temples of Smyrna or the sculptures of Pergamos. No springs exhaled intoxicating vapors to shroud it in the awe that hallowed Hierapolis. No mythical traditions clothed it in the sacred livery of Ephesus and Eleusis. No monarch of renown like the founder of Antioch had emptied his treasury by enduing it with splendors to perpetuate his memory. Yet for more than two centuries this insignificant city enjoyed a celebrity wider probably than Bethlehem had gained before the birth of Constantine or Mecca before that of Amrou. A single event was the cradle of its fame.

About the time when Joseph went up to be enrolled with Mary, his espoused wife, — for aught we know on the night when the angels sang to the shepherds, — Tyana gave birth to a marvelous man, a man for whose worship many temples were erected before a single building had been raised in any part of the world for the worship of Christ. The man's name was Apollonius, and the place of his birth became his surname, so that he was called "Apollonius of Tyana," as

the Saviour from the home of his childhood was known as " Jesus of Nazareth."

This man is the unsolved puzzle of
historians. All concede that his fascinating and mysterious personality filled
an immense space in the early centuries,
and that his influence was incalculably
great; but in their judgment of his character and the source of his influence I
have found no two writers in complete
agreement, and few who do not appear
to doubt their own conclusions. Between
the worshipers of Apollonius, or rather
between the worshipers of the mysterious
being who passed for Apollonius and the
worshipers of Christ, the subtlest and
most significant spiritual conflict of the
first three centuries was waged. In it
the pagan prophet appeared for a time
to have won the victory, though in fact
he had only prepared the way before the
face of our Saviour.

To describe that conflict is the purpose of this paper.

The reports of Apollonius which have
reached us fall into three groups, —
facts, probabilities, and fictions. The
facts are few, the probabilities are important, the fictions, though incredible,
are significant, because they harmonize
completely with the facts and the probabilities.

I. We know how the man looked.
His undoubted portrait preserved on
coin or medal is familiar to scholars.
The august face is bearded and crowned
with laurel as Christ was crowned with
thorns. The features are Greek and suggest "the front of Jove himself." But
for the winning sweetness and gentleness
in the curves of the lips the face might
pass for the original of Neri's Jupiter
Tonans.

It is worthy of remark that the countenance of this inscrutable enigma should

have been so carefully preserved and so
generally forgotten while no line of sculpture or drawing exists that gives the faint-
est hint of the appearance of Him who
in so many million homes is loved as an
elder brother.

We know that Apollonius was enrolled among the gods; that temples in
various places were built for his worship,
and that for a long though indefinite
period he was the object of devout
adoration. Early in the third century
Caracalla visited Tyana, built and conse-
crated a temple to him there, granted
the right of Roman citizenship to the
inhabitants of the place, and constituted
it a "sacred city." Not many years later
Alexander Severus put the statue of
Apollonius in his private oratory. The
implacable Aurelian, though exasperated
by the obstinacy with which Tyana had
opposed his arms, when, after a sternly
resisted siege, he captured it, treated the

inhabitants with distinguished honor and shed no blood except that of the traitor who betrayed the city into his hands. There is no plausible explanation of a clemency unparalleled elsewhere in the career of that cruel conqueror, except the explanation made by himself, that he obeyed the command given him in a vision by Apollonius.

It is certain that at the request of the Empress Domna, the mother of Caracalla, Philostratos wrote a book which some call a religious novel with Apollonius for its hero, which others call his " Memorabilia," but which his disciples regarded as " the Gospel of Apollonius," precisely as we name the writings of the evangelists the " Gospels " or " Good News " of Christ. The impossibility of distinguishing sharply the facts from the fictions in this book has veiled in impenetrable mist the personality of its hero.

II. The probabilities. The evidence in hand leaves no reasonable doubt that Apollonius was not only a man of commanding genius, but that he was also a character entitled, by purity of purpose and unselfish desire to bless his fellowmen both by deeds of beneficence and by giving them truer conceptions of deity and duty, to be classed with Socrates and almost with St. Paul. Though this seems to me certain, I put it among the probabilities because one or two writers of repute count him only the best among that herd of self-seeking thaumaturgists who thronged the first centuries.

A collection of his letters said to have been made by Hadrian still exists, but critics are at odds about them. Whether all of them, or some of them, or none of them are genuine cannot be determined. It seems certain that he was personally known to Vespasian and Titus, the two most excellent emperors between Augustus and Trajan, and it is probable that he exerted an appreciable influence upon their policies. It seems indubitable that, probably without knowing whence the influence came, he was himself powerfully influenced by the teachings of Christ. He was educated first at Tarsus and afterward at Ægæ, very near that place. It is therefore not incredible that he met Paul, perhaps saw him frequently, for the two boys, though one was a Jew and the other a Gentile, were both aristocrats, each of them hungered after righteousness, and each of them had that gift of keen observation which nothing worth noting in mice or men escapes.

III. The improbabilities. These, though incredible to us, were believed by his disciples as sincerely as the majority of Christians to-day credit the miracles of Christ. I cull a few of them from that fascinating book which may be named

" The Gospel of Apollonius according to Philostratos."

It would be superfluous to point out the resemblances they bear to the facts in our Saviour's life.

Apollonius had no mortal father, but was born to an invisible deity. Swans sang over his cradle songs which proclaimed the advent of a Saviour. When a child he was taken by his parents to Tarsus, where the learned doctors welcomed him. Repelled by the wickedness of that splendid city, he begged and obtained permission from his parents to retire into the quiet village of Ægæ. Here he grew up in obscurity, finding favor with God and man. The rest of his life he spent going about doing good, teaching, healing, comforting those that mourned. Though the heart of his instruction was that men should love their neighbors as themselves and practice self-denial for the benefit of their fellows, he

seems to have escaped all taint of that
vicious notion which had infected the
whole pagan world, and was beginning to
distemper Christianity with the belief
that it is meritorious to do disagreeable
things merely because one hates to. He
would go through fire to rescue the
burning, but he would not walk on nails
for no other reason than that they hurt.

On one occasion at Ephesus a flock
of sparrows lighted on a tree near the
place where he was preaching. Presently
another sparrow flew to them, uttering a
peculiar cry, whereupon they all darted
off together. "Watch the sparrows," he
exclaimed, "and learn from them. That
little bird has found some grain, and instead of trying to eat it all himself has
called his fellows to share his wealth. If
you did the same you would be called
spendthrifts." With that he ended his
sermon and sent his hearers to "consider
the sparrows." They found the birds

feasting upon wheat which a boy in the street had spilled from his basket.

At Rome he met a procession bearing to the grave the body of a nobleman's young daughter. He bade the bearers set down the bier, touched the corpse, and spoke a few words in a low voice. Immediately the maid opened her eyes, arose, and returned to her father's house, "as Alcestis did of old when recalled to life by Hercules." Her relatives gave him a thank offering of one hundred and fifty thousand drachmas, which he settled upon the damsel for a marriage portion.

The manner of his departure from this world is variously reported, but all accounts agree that it was not by death. After his translation a young man who did not believe in the immortality of the soul, and was preaching a crusade against those who did, visited Tyana. There Apollonius appeared to him, convinced him of his error, told him many things

of the life to come, and sent him forth
an eloquent advocate of the doctrine he
had before denounced.

Most of the teachings attributed by
Philostratos to Apollonius savor of the
New Testament. But to the New Tes-
tament they

" Are as moonlight unto sunlight, and as water unto
wine."

Which of them were uttered by the sage,
and which were coined by his biographer,
it is not possible to say. Those, however,
whom Dr. Bushnell has failed to con-
vince that the character portrayed in the
gospels is beyond the power of the human imagination to invent, will probably
find their doubts dissolved by a comparison of Philostratos with Matthew, Mark,
or Luke. Philostratos possessed super-
lative culture, high moral sensibility, and
great literary skill. He had to help him a
very considerable familiarity with the sayings of Christ. Yet in trying to present

a perfect character he has painted an ideal which before Jesus of Nazareth flickers as a thieved and gutted candle brought into sunlight.

There is no evidence that Apollonius trained disciples or attempted to found a new school of either philosophy or religion. He seems to have "gone about doing good," trying to learn and to teach the truth without thinking of his reputation or taking consciously any measures to perpetuate his influence. After his death, however, his fame grew steadily. Early in the third century, when he had long been worshiped, his influence was immensely increased by the act of a broken-hearted woman. This is the story : —

There lived at Emesa two sisters. They were Syrian peasants. Their names were Domna and Mæsa. They worshiped the sun, and both of them seem to have been attached in some

capacity to the famous temple of that
divinity in their city. Domna had gained
celebrity for skill in astrology. A certain
widowed Roman general, a firm believer
in that pseudo-science, hearing that her
horoscope had marked her as the wife
of an emperor, sought out and married
her.

This general, the most gifted captain
of his age, cold, crafty, cruel, not like
Caligula with the cruelty of fitful passion,
but like Napoleon with the cruelty of
deliberate policy, unscrupulous, superstitious, and insatiably ambitious, became
in 193 A. D. by usurpation the Emperor
Septimius Severus. No small part of his
eminent achievements were due to his
wife, Domna, the peasant girl. She was
a woman of rare genius, strong will, and
ambition, almost equal to her husband's.
But she possessed what he lacked, a
heart. Her character was not good. In
our day it would seem extremely bad.

But for a Roman empress in her time it served well enough, and could not well be criticised by society which had accepted Caligula as god and Faustina as madonna. For a time husband and wife lived in close amity, each leaning upon the talents of the other. They had two sons, Caracalla and Geta. But time, which generally brings trouble to families where selfishness usurps the place of affection, had to be reckoned with. A favorite of the emperor, named Plautianus, jealous of Domna's influence, filled her husband's ears with slanders of his wife; made him believe that she had planned to poison him. Her two sons, both coveting the crown, hated each other with a deadly hatred. She tried with all her power to reconcile them, but her efforts only made it more evident that each of them was determined to assassinate his brother. Their father, compelled to leave Rome for Britain, took both sons with him because he dared not leave them behind. He died at York, probably poisoned by the elder of the two. They brought the ashes of their parent home. On the way neither dared to eat a morsel or drink a drop from the other's hand that had not been tested and proved free of poison. At Rome mother and sons, each of the latter protected by an armed guard from the dagger of his brother, celebrated the apotheosis of husband and father. When the obsequies were over the widow called into the closet of her grief the two boys who were to share the throne between them, and said : —

"You find means, my sons, to divide the earth and the seas between you, and the streams between them, you say, divide the two continents. But how will you be able to divide your mother? How am I, your unhappy parent, to be torn asunder and shared between you both?

There is but one way. First, sheathe your swords in my breast and then let my body be cut in two, that each prince may bury half his mother in his own territory. So shall I be equally parted between you together with your empire of earth and sea."

Though Domna may not have expressed her anguish in precisely these words which Herodian attributes to her, there is no doubt that they give a true conception of her despair; for Herodian was a contemporary, an honest reporter, and knew whereof he affirmed.

The mother's pleadings were futile. Caracalla, hiding Macbeth's treachery beneath Iago's hypocrisy, persuaded her to invite his younger brother to meet him in her private chamber for a friendly conference. There he had concealed assassins who stabbed Geta in her arms while she vainly strove to make her body a shield against their daggers.

Nor was this the bitterest drop in her cup. After the cruel deed had been done, because the anguish in her face inspired the sympathy of courtiers, the fratricide, by threats that if she refused to obey him he would slay her with the same weapon that had pierced the heart of her son, compelled her to put on gay garments, to dance, and to sing.

"When it is dark *enough* the stars come out." It is not strange that in the horror of this great darkness the tortured woman gazed eagerly upon the only star that shone in her sky. We are told that she sought consolation in philosophy; that she spent whole days with its professors.

For nearly two centuries the words of Him who came into the world to "heal the brokenhearted" had been slowly but surely penetrating to wider and yet wider horizons. Christianity was still the religion of the poor and the lowly, but the teachings of Christ had permeated the air. They had been whispered in kitchens, shouted from the stakes of martyrs, scoffed at in palaces, murmured in hovels. Executioners had marveled to see them give rest to the tortured and courage to cowards. Slaves had seen them transform ferocious masters into sympathetic friends, and masters had seen them change truculent slaves into obedient servants. Pagan philosophers had vainly endeavored to explain how a superstition which seemed to them absurd could plant and foster honesty in thieves, kindness in professional assassins, generosity in misers, and valor in poltroons. But the facts were obvious and indubitable. Trajan, who had striven more zealously than any other Cæsar for the strict enforcement of established law, had recognized them and wrenched the law till it cracked to conform to them. He had ordered Pliny to shut his eyes when

Christians refused to pour libations, and to disregard accusations unconfirmed by their own confessions.

Thus the words of Christ penetrated all atmospheres. Domna had heard, but thought little of them in the days of her pride when her heart was whole. But when her heart was broken they came to her with power, though she knew not whence they came. Many of them were credited to Apollonius. His was a household name among the rich and the mighty, as was the name of Christ among the poor and the needy. Some of Christ's teachings Apollonius had repeated, others he was believed to have originated. To Domna Christ was at best an obscure foreigner who had lived in the slums and been ignominiously gibbeted. Apollonius was a distinct and deified personality, admired by philosophers and worshiped by aristocrats. Hungry for help, she commissioned Philostratos to collect all that could be learned of him. Thus the famous book came to be written, and a poor parody of our Saviour's life became the gospel of the Roman court. But the diluted gospel and the tinseled Christ were insufficient. For a time they did some service. It was doubtless Domna's influence that sent her dastard son to Tyana and constrained him to build a temple and consecrate the city to the sham saviour, for in spite of his atrocity Caracalla appears to have given his mother all the affection it was in the power of his fiendish nature to bestow. But the sham saviour could not give the despairing woman the blessedness of them that mourn, for she died a suicide. Yet she lived until, through her influence, the worship of Apollonius had received a strong impulse and been put upon the way toward becoming the imperial religion. That road was closed to it and opened to Christianity by the in-

fluence of another and a very different
woman, whose story runs parallel to
hers.

Domna's sister Mæsa had two daughters, cousins therefore of Caracalla and
Geta. Their names were Soemis and Mamæa. Each of them bore a son and each
of the sons became an emperor. The son
of Soemis was surpassingly beautiful.
While still a boy he was made a priest
of the Sun. His splendid appearance
fascinated the soldiers, and by the machinations of his mother he was placed upon
the throne of the Cæsars. There he disgraced humanity by an ostentatious depravity which exceeded the obscenities of
Nero, and had no trace of those artistic
qualities which make it possible to believe that even Nero was once a man.
In less than four years this son, the Emperor Heliogabalus, with his mother,
perished at the hands of an exasperated
soldiery and an outraged people, who

murdered them and threw their bodies into the Tiber.

The son of Mamæa met a different fate. His mother had in some way been drawn to Christianity. Perhaps it was only that she clung to the best there was in the religion fostered by her aunt Domna, and was by that led toward the light. However that may be, she adopted the principles of Christ and trained her son to obey them.

Now there was at Alexandria one of the wisest, devoutest, and most persuasive Christians who have ever lived. In knowledge of the Scriptures no one equaled him, in classical learning no one excelled him, in powers of persuasion no one approached him. His name was Origen. Before her son's character was fully formed, and probably to confirm convictions which had already nearly, if not wholly, mastered her, she sent for this man. He spent a considerable time with her. It cannot be doubted that all his matchless abilities were strained to lead her into a deeper devotion to Christ. Her conduct shows that he succeeded. Her conceptions of life and its duties were antipodal to those of her mother and her sister. In place of the diabolical ambition which ruined the other members of her family, there appeared in her a genuine patriotism. Before her son was fifteen the army forced Elagabalus, who had just failed in an attempt to murder him, to appoint him successor to the throne. Mamæa guarded her boy with wise and tender care. She surrounded him with the best and ablest men in Rome. Without taking him out of the world, her resolute will and motherly tact kept him from the evil and prepared him for the high place to which Providence had called him.

When he became emperor under the name of Alexander Severus, the court was immediately reformed. A change more instantaneous than that which, when William took the helm that James had fled from, swept Jeffreys from the chancellorship and drove Claverhouse into exile, renovated Rome. The great jurists whom Elagabalus had dismissed that he might fill their places with men selected from the gutters, the race-course, and the arena, for no other reason than their bull necks and brawny breasts and bestial proclivities, were recalled to office. Papinian, the greatest jurist Rome ever produced, had been murdered by Caracalla because when commanded to palliate before the Senate Geta's assassination he replied that it was easier to commit fratricide than to justify it; but Ulpian and Paulus still lived and gave lustre to the new administration.

Severus sought counsel from the best men in the empire, and was swayed by their advice, but to the close of his life his mother was his chief and most trusted guide. Abuses were corrected, morals were purified. Nine years of peaceful prosperity followed his accession, during all of which the example of a family Christian in all but name was given to the Roman world by the relations between the emperor and his mother; and though the last five of the fourteen years of his beneficent reign were agitated by wars which the wickedness of former rulers had made inevitable, they were wars which proved that the influence which made him just and gentle in peace had also made him brave and generous in war.

This upright man, devoted son, and beneficent sovereign placed in his private oratory four statues. They represented Orpheus, Abraham, Apollonius, and Jesus of Nazareth. To our minds this may seem an inexplicable combination. What relation has Orpheus to

Abraham or Apollonius to Christ? we naturally ask. But had we lived in Rome at the court of Alexander, the grouping would have seemed to us appropriate, and would have told us a plain and most impressive fact.

Orpheus had long been accepted by Pythagoreans as the one whose resurrection proved immortality; whose lyre showed that persuasion is more powerful than force; whose rescue of Eurydice proclaimed the victory of self-sacrificing love over all things, even over death. The members of the Orphic societies, though few in number, were the salt of the heathen world. Their white garments were a protest against the scarlet splendors of pagan debauchery. Their ascetic rules, which forbade the use of animal food, and cultivated plain living and high thinking, were a perpetual rebuke to the purple and fine linen of those who fared sumptuously every day and did nothing else. They had done much to prepare the way before Apollonius, who had himself been a Pythagorean or was believed to have been one. As Christ was the ultimate fruit of all the good which had grown for centuries in Judæa, Apollonius was the consummation of the best that Greece and Rome had been able to produce. As Orpheus passed for the spiritual ancestor of Apollonius, Abraham bore a similar relation to Christ. Such was the reasoning. The idea of the unity of God had not yet mastered the Gentile mind. That there should be two divinities with equal claims to worship would not seem strange to Romans.

The strongest trait in Alexander's character was family affection. It had kept him loyal to Elagabalus in spite of that monster's unspeakable infamy, in spite of the monster's attempt to murder him. At a time when no one could oppose the will of the army without risking his life, it had kept him from yielding a hair's breadth to the clamors of an infuriated soldiery bent on forcing him to usurp his cousin's throne. For many years the strong will of his great-aunt Domna had been the controlling influence in his family. What then could be more natural than that reverence for her should lead him to place the statue of the god she had taught him to revere beside the image of the God his mother had taught him to worship?

However this may be, in his oratory Christianity was for the first time raised before the whole Roman Empire to an equality with the loftiest cult of paganism. It might still be hated, it might still be fought, — and so it was at intervals for a hundred years, — but it could never again be, as it had been, despised. In a century almost to the year from the day on which Alexander put the statue of

Jesus beside that of Apollonius, Constantine placed the Cross above the eagles and made Christianity legally the religion of the empire.

Gradually the gospel according to Philostratos, the splendid rhetorician, faded from human memory, and the gospels according to the despised publican, the obscure disciple, the faithful physician, and the humble fisherman whom Jesus loved became the Bible of our race. For this we are indebted to the afflictions of Domna and the influence of Mamæa more than to the battle of the Milvian; to the unrecorded words of Origen whispered in the closet more than to the obtrusive sword of Constantine, and the *in hoc signo* trumpeted at the street corners of the world.

The Riverside Press

Electrotyped and printed by H. O. Houghton & Co.
Cambridge, Mass., U. S. A.